Y0-CAB-049

Discovering the Nineteenth Century

759.4
PISSARRO

Christopher Lloyd

CAMILLE
PISSARRO

HINSDALE PUBLIC LIBRARY
HINSDALE, IL 60521

DEDICATED IN GRATITUDE TO
THE MEMORY OF G.H.R.N.

Frontispiece:
Landscape at Saint-Charles, 1891.

Design on the binding from the
righthand figure on a study sheet
with two female harvesters, 1882.
Black chalk. (BL 123)
Ashmolean Museum, Oxford

© 1981 by Editions d'Art Albert Skira S.A., Geneva
This edition published in the United States of America in 1981 by

*R*IZZOLI INTERNATIONAL PUBLICATIONS, INC.
712 Fifth Avenue/ New York 10019

All rights reserved.
No parts of this book may be reproduced
in any manner whatsoever without permission
Library of Congress Catalog Card Number: 81–51312
ISBN: 0–8478–0391–0
Printed in Switzerland

Contents

"I was studying Camille Pissarro the other day. There is no other painter who is so conscientious, so exact. He is one of the naturalists who confronts nature head on. And yet his canvases always have a character which is quite their own: a note of austerity and a truly heroic grandeur. You might look out for his incomparable landscapes, they are quite unlike any others. They are supremely personal and totally convincing."

Emile Zola, *Mon Salon*, from the section entitled *Les Paysagistes*, originally published in *L'Evénement Illustré*, 19 May 1868.

"Nothing of novelty or of excellence appeared that Pissarro had not been among the first, if not the very first, to discern and to defend."

Thadée Natanson, *Peints à leur tour*, Paris, 1948.

Coconut Palms by the Sea, St. Thomas, 1856.

*View of Charlotte Amalie,
St. Thomas, 1851.
Lithograph by Tegner and Kittendorff
after a painting by Fritz Melbye.*

St. Thomas and Venezuela

CAMILLE PISSARRO spent most of his early life in one of the more exotic parts of the world. He was born on 10 July 1830 at Charlotte Amalie, the principal town on the island of St. Thomas in the Lesser Antilles. The family was Jewish and Portuguese by origin, from Braganza, but in the middle of the eighteenth century Pissarro's ancestors had settled in Bordeaux. It was from Bordeaux in 1824 that his father, Frédéric, sailed to St. Thomas to act as executor of his uncle's will. The uncle, Isaac Petit, was in fact only related by marriage, but Frédéric took full responsibility for the haberdashery business run by the Petit family by remaining on the island and, indeed, in 1826, in slightly scandalous circumstances for that time, married Isaac Petit's widow, Rachel, who was seven years his senior. Frédéric and Rachel Pissarro had four sons in all, Camille being the second surviving son, registered at birth as Jacob Abraham Pizzarro. As their business interests expanded, so the shop over which they lived began to stock general merchandise. It was apparent that at first Frédéric's sons were expected to assist him in the family business before one of them took it over completely. This role was eventually shared by Camille's elder brother, Alfred, and his half-brother-in-law, Phineas Isaacson, although after Frédéric's retirement to Paris and death in 1865 the business in St. Thomas began to devolve upon those members of the Petit family remaining on the island. In short, the Pissarro family returned to France where Camille, who was the first to tire of St. Thomas, was to establish himself as a painter of European significance.

These details of Pissarro family history are not uncharacteristic of the fate of the island of St. Thomas itself. The years spent at Charlotte Amalie and later in Venezuela were formative ones for the young artist and it is necessary to examine the ambience in which he developed in order to gain a proper understanding of his art. It is no exaggeration to say that Pissarro observed his surroundings in St. Thomas and in Venezuela closely and that this was a determining factor in his later development.

St. Thomas is the largest of the Virgin Islands, a group in the Lesser Antilles discovered by Christopher Columbus in 1493 on his second voyage to the New World. Subsequently, the island changed hands between English, Dutch and Spanish settlers until in 1671 it was finally settled by the Danes. By the mid-eighteenth century St. Thomas was declared a free port and this marked the beginning of its prosperity. There were two comparatively short periods during the Napoleonic wars when St. Thomas was occupied by the British, but it was restored to the Danish government in 1815 until the island was finally ceded to the United States of America in 1917. A local historian of the island, John Knox, writing in 1852, describes St. Thomas as being thirteen miles long and three miles wide with a population of 13,666, the majority of whom lived in the town of Charlotte Amalie. The island flourished during the first half of the nineteenth century solely on account of the port, but its prosperity was relatively shortlived. An English writer, C. Washington Eves, wrote in *The West Indies* published in 1889 under the auspices of The Royal Colonial Institute: "For many years, until quite recently, it [St. Thomas] was of much importance as a depot for the mail steamers and an entrepôt of trade for the islands. It owed this position to its extremely convenient situation. It was like a key to the West Indies, and certainly the most convenient centre… for the distribution inter-colonially of passengers and goods… Between 1850 and 1873 the demand for goods of every kind was very great for distribution in the above countries [West Indies and South America], and fortunes were rapidly realised. Charlotte Amalie became one of the busiest towns in the Western Tropics, and in providing amusement and spending money not at all the most backward. But soon after 1870 the great advance which steam had made in lessening the importance of entrepôts, and going straight to consuming countries, began to tell upon St. Thomas, and signs of decadence appeared. The construction of telegraph poles was also detrimental to the business of an intermediary port."

The years 1870-1880, therefore, saw a rapid decline in trade and the old commercial importance of St. Thomas disappeared. Eves concluded that "the island remains in a condition of mourning over its past importance and prosperity." It can be seen from this brief outline of the history of St. Thomas that Frédéric Pissarro's arrival on the island in 1824 and his death in 1865 coincided with its most prosperous years. In fact, Camille Pissarro lived on the island in its heyday and his art developed in the context of commercial enterprise.

The geographical significance of St. Thomas helps to explain why there are so many first-hand accounts of the island. These again form a backcloth against which Camille Pissarro's earliest works must be seen. Eves in his report of 1889 asserts that "many thousands of European visitors to the West Indies and South America during the last half-century have involuntarily made acquaintance with it, and while they have admitted its beauty… yet they were not sorry to get away again, for it has always had the reputation of being unhealthy." As early as 1819-1820 another English writer, George Laval Chesterton, who sailed to South America to observe the wars of independence, referred to St. Thomas as "a place of resort for all the outcasts of other islands, where every nefarious species of commerce is tolerated, and where men of most desperate characters and fortunes are assembled… The island is barren and utterly destitute of water; the rain water is therefore caught in tanks, and there being so many of the latter, causes great swarms of mosquitoes." Eves, however, stated more scientifically that there was no current in the land-locked harbour and no system of drainage, so that the water stagnated. Yet, although provision was later made for drainage of the harbour, the death rate from tropical fever remained high.

The most famous account of St. Thomas occurs in Anthony Trollope's *The West Indies and the Spanish Main* (1859) which was regarded by the author as his best book. Trollope undertook the journey on behalf of the General Post Office for whom he then worked. His account was published a mere four years after Camille Pissarro left the island for good. It is an ebullient description, highly critical, but not totally oblivious to the island's charms. "Let it be understood by all men,"

Trollope declares, "that in these latitudes the respectable, comfortable, well-to-do route from every place to every other place is via the little Danish island of St. Thomas." He describes it as an emporium, "a depot for cigars, light dresses, brandy, boots, and Eau-de-Cologne. Many men therefore of many nations go thither to make money." Indeed, Trollope admits, "I must imagine what good can accrue to a man at St. Thomas if it be not the good of amassing money. It is one of the hottest and one of the most unhealthy spots among all these hot and unhealthy regions." The people, according to Trollope, form a "Hispano-Dano-Niggery-Yankee-doodle population." Yet, there are compensating factors: one is the setting. "Seen from the water St. Thomas is very pretty. It is not so much the scenery of the island that pleases as the aspect of the town itself. It stands on three hills or mounts, with higher hills, green to their summit, rising behind them. Each mount is topped by a pleasant, cleanly edifice, and pretty-looking houses stretch down the sides to the water's edge. The buildings do look pretty and nice, and as though chance had arranged them for a picture. Indeed, as seen from the harbour, the town looks like a panorama exquisitely painted. The air is thin and transparent, and every line shows itself clearly. As seen the town of St. Thomas is certainly attractive. But it is like the Dead Sea fruit; all the charm is gone when it is tasted. Land there, and the beauty vanishes." Clearly, St. Thomas was not Prospero's isle. Rather, it was a pawn on the chess board of history.

Trollope's description, as well as his criticisms, were probably not dissimilar to Camille Pissarro's own reactions to St. Thomas. The young painter was certainly aware of the shortcomings of remaining on the island and he seems to have been eager to leave it as soon as possible. The detailed summary provided by Knox of the facilities on the island shows that there was little to entice a young man, whatever his vocation, to stay. Slavery may have been abolished and religious toleration widely practised, but, on the other hand, there were no proper schools and "no places of amusement." Pissarro was therefore sent to a school in Paris at Passy, near the Bois de Boulogne, for six years (1841-1847) and on his return had to wait until 1852 before escaping

for two years to Venezuela with the Danish artist, Fritz Melbye. Just over a year after returning to St. Thomas from Venezuela, Camille, generously released from the family business by his elder brother, Alfred, left for France for good. Yet, Pissarro did not spurn the chances offered by the island completely, since while he was there the young artist drew constantly. Indeed, the subject matter of the drawings might be said to illustrate Trollope's account of St. Thomas in a remarkable way.

Pissarro's early work is dominated by his drawings. This is not to say that his œuvre is devoid of paintings, but of those that do survive most are dated after his departure for France in 1855 where he continued to paint subjects inspired by St. Thomas or Venezuela. By contrast, there are numerous drawings dating from between 1851 and 1855, perhaps reflecting the informal and sporadic instruction that he had received while at school at Passy. Here, according to an early biographer, a succession of headmasters included art classes in the curriculum and apparently spotted Pissarro's talent for drawing. M. Savary, for instance, who was headmaster at the time of Pissarro's arrival, had a relative, Auguste, whose work was frequently accepted at the Salon between 1824 and 1859. Auguste Savary was principally, it seems, a landscape painter. Almost prophetically he painted views in Mayenne, the area in northwest France where Pissarro frequently worked during the mid-1870s. Unfortunately, none of Savary's works can at present be located and therefore it is difficult to ascertain what positive influence, if any, he might have exerted on the youthful Pissarro. It is certain, however, that Pissarro's innate ability as a draughtsman was encouraged at M. Savary's school and probably disciplined by indirect reference to academic procedures. The first dated drawings occur in 1851, the favoured medium being pencil often reworked in pen and ink and occasionally heightened with watercolour. These drawings are tentative in style and somewhat uniform in texture. The lines are usually short and broken, almost crinkly; hatching is often reinforced with the pen; the watercolour almost dabbed on to the paper with small stabs of the brush. The subjects provide a visual record of Pissarro's life on St. Thomas extending

Route de Bussy, St. Thomas, 1852. Pencil.

St. Thomas, c. 1852. Watercolour over pencil.

Lovers' Meeting, 1852-1854. Pen and ink over pencil.

Sheet of Studies of Watercarriers. Pen and ink over pencil.

Samuel Prout (1783-1852).
Plate 15 from Microcosm, *1841. Lithograph.*

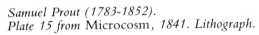

Samuel Prout (1783-1852).
Plate 19 from Easy Lessons in Landscape Drawing, *1819. Lithograph.*

from topographical views to sheets of figure studies depicting the daily routine of the islanders. Some of these drawings were compositional and were presumably the artist's first attempts at devising paintings, although none has survived. Two stylistic features of these drawings indicate how Pissarro might have developed his interest in drawing in isolation on St. Thomas. The fine pen lines, the shading with parallel lines and the small dense areas of cross hatching make up a style closely related to printmaking, to etching and to wood engraving in particular. These affinities suggest that Pissarro might have had access to popular journals and illustrated magazines, such as *L'Illustration* and *Le Magasin pittoresque*, which abounded in visual images to stimulate a young artist. Similarly, the crowding of the page with numerous figures might indicate that Pissarro had perused some of the wide range of drawing manuals that were published by English and French artists during the first half of the nineteenth century. Samuel Prout's *Microcosm* (1841) is an apposite example, just as in some of the landscape drawings the clusters of short intricate pencil lines resemble the lithographs in Prout's *Easy Lessons in Landscape Drawing* (1819). Prout's publications need not be the exact examples that Pissarro consulted, since a host of such titles was prepared by other artists like the brothers Newton and Theodore Fielding or James Duffield Harding, but it is reasonable to assert that Pissarro's early drawings reflect works of this type which were widely known in France. It is, however, harder to discover how Pissarro would have obtained popular or specialized publications on which to feed his talent. The local historian, Knox, records that St. Thomas established a Reading Room and Library in 1839: "The tables of the reading room are well supplied with periodicals, pamphlets, and newspapers from Europe and the United States." If the local library did not supply the works of Prout and others, then it is possible that Pissarro could have brought copies from France in 1847 when he left school, or, alternatively, have been given them by Fritz Melbye.

Melbye is an important link in Pissarro's early career. He was able to give advice and therefore provide an added sense of direction to Pissarro's art. Indeed, in so far as Pissarro had an artistic education, Melbye may be said to have completed it. The difficulty was that the pupil rapidly outstripped the master. Melbye was, in fact, only four years older than Pissarro, but he had an established reputation and had already gained important commissions. It was most probably a commission from the Danish government that brought him to the Lesser Antilles in 1849. Melbye was an itinerant artist returning at brief intervals to Europe before settling temporarily in New York, eventually dying in Shanghai in 1896. Like his elder brother, Anton, who worked in Paris, Fritz Melbye specialized in landscape and marine painting. Anton Melbye had studied under Christoffer Wilhelm Eckersberg at the Academy of Fine Arts in Copenhagen, one of the numerous academies that flourished during the first half of the nineteenth century in Europe. It is likely that Fritz Melbye's style was nurtured by his elder brother and that under his influence he rapidly became an efficient and capable painter of landscapes and marine subjects. Pissarro met Fritz Melbye on St. Thomas sometime in 1851 and in October 1852 the two artists (their common language being English) left the island for a visit to Venezuela where Pissarro remained until August 1854. It is in Venezuela that Melbye's short-lived influence on Pissarro is most clearly discernible. Fortunately, a considerable amount of work by both artists has survived, thereby affording some direct comparisons, particularly as regards drawings.

From the turn of the eighteenth and nineteenth centuries European interest in South American countries grew. Partly this was the result of political events as individual countries sought independence from the Iberian peninsula and partly it was scientific curiosity. There are numerous published accounts of visits made to the continent frequently combining summaries of the campaigns of Simón Bolívar with descriptions of tropical forests and vegetation. Most European visitors had read, and often allude to, Alexander von Humboldt's extensive classic publication on his explorations in South America amounting to some thirty volumes (Paris, 1805-1834). During this period and again after 1850 there followed a vast expansion of literature on South America including Venezuela. Some of these sources, as for St. Thomas, again provide valuable information on the country that Melbye and Pissarro reached after a short sea voyage on 12 November 1852.

Edward Sullivan in *Rambles and Scrambles in North and South America* (1852) was especially enamoured of the variety of riches presented by Venezuela. "It is a great pity Venezuela is so much out of the high roads of travellers, and that the inconveniences of getting at it are so great. It is, in my opinion, the most beautiful country, as regards climate, scenery, and productions in the world. The inhabitants are intelligent, civil, and honest, and although there is no excessive wealth in the country, there is, on the other hand, no great poverty, and actual want is unknown, where beef can be procured to any amount for halfpenny a pound, and plantains and bananas for nothing. The inns are excellent, and travelling perfectly safe. You may, on the sides of its precipitous valleys, in a few hours, ascend from the productions of the torrid zone to those of the frigid. You may, if you like, dine off beefsteak and potatoes, cooled down with French claret or real London stout; or, if you prefer it, you may, in imitation of Leo X and the Emperor Vitellius, feast your guests on joints of monkey and jaguar, and have your entremets of parrots' tongues and humming birds' breasts, washed down with sparkling pulque, tapped from the graceful mughay growing at your very door." This may read like a travel brochure, but it faithfully reflects the European reaction to a tropical country that is commonly found in other writers.

Melbye and Pissarro landed on the Venezuelan coast at the harbour of La Guaira. Humboldt described La Guaira as " a roadstead, then a port. The sea is constantly agitated, and the ships suffer at once by the actions of the wind, the tideways, the bad anchorage, and the worms." Every traveller refers to the discomfiture of landing at La Guaira. Unlike St. Thomas, it was not a landlocked harbour and Melbye's painting of the subject shows how rough the sea could be. The artists spent about one month in La Guaira concentrating upon topographical views. The town itself was exceptional, owing to the backcloth of steep mountains, as portrayed by Sir Robert Ker Porter in 1825. "There are scarcely two or three hundred yards flat ground

View of La Guaira by "G.T." Lithograph.

View of La Guaira from Maiquetia, 1852-1854. Pen and ink over pencil.

Camino Nuevo de Caracas. Pen and ink over pencil.

between this mighty wall and the ocean," wrote Sullivan. "Owing to its peculiar position at the foot of these rocky mountains, which never get thoroughly cooled, but radiate more or less caloric continually night and day, and owing to the sea breezes being little felt, La Guayra is, without exception, the hottest place in the western hemisphere." The mountains, or, more strictly, cordillera of the Andes, overlooking La Guaira were called the Silla, whilst the ridge separating the coast from Caracas was the Cerro de Avila. La Guaira, therefore, really had very little to offer the two artists. Humboldt had not been impressed by it either: "The aspect of this place has something solitary and gloomy; we seemed not to be on a continent, covered with vast forests, but in a rocky island, destitute of mould and vegetation. With the exception of Cape Blanco and the cocoa-trees of Maiquetia, no view meets the eye but that of the horizon, the sea, and the azure vault of Heaven. The heat is stifling during the day, and most frequently during the night."

Melbye and Pissarro made drawings of the harbour, the fortifications and the neighbouring parts of the shoreline before moving on, as everyone did, to Caracas. They were established in the city by December 1852 in a house near the Plaza Major which was to serve as their base for the next two years.

The route from La Guaira to Caracas before the introduction of the railway was spectacular and Pissarro made at least two drawings of it. An anonymous American writer recorded in 1858 for *Harper's New Monthly Magazine:* "The distance from La Guayra as the bird flies is six miles; as the donkey twists and zigzags along the path which the Indians followed untold centuries back, and their Spanish conquerors after them, over the mountain… it is about twelve miles, taking from three to five hours' time, according to the quality of your beast. There is another route unknown to birds or donkeys…, the camino nuevo. This is a cart-track over which an Italian vetturino ventures, in fine weather, for the benefit of such travellers as are willing to risk being broken on a wheel rather than be shaken to pieces on a mule." Such was the road along which Melbye and Pissarro travelled and which they depicted. The road led over the Avila ridge to Caracas and afforded some relief to those travellers who were troubled by the heat at La Guaira. George Laval Chesterton in *A Narrative of Proceedings in Venezuela, in South America, in the years 1819 and 1820* described the route as follows: "The ascent, though steep, is not difficult, as it is paved with small stones, and kept in repair, there being a constant thoroughfare of mules and horses. The air strikes astonishingly cold as one approaches the top, and the water is constantly dripping from the trees, even though there has been no rain for a considerable time."

Apart from changing atmosphere, the road provided spectacular views of the sea on one side and, eventually, on the other, of the valley of Chacao in which Caracas lies. According to Sullivan, "The valley of Chacao is about thirty miles in length and some nine or ten in breadth. It is… the most fertile spot in the world, producing in equal profusion the grains and fruits of Europe, and the sugar-cane and plantain of the tropics. The valley is well watered by the Rio La Guayra, which meanders through the centre." This sight impressed most travellers and both Melbye and Pissarro responded to it. The writer in *Harper's New Monthly Magazine* gives a more detailed description: "Looked down upon from the mountain, Caracas, with its flat-tiled roofs, has the appearance of a brick-yard surrounded by a garden, the only noticeable break in its uniformity being one white cathedral and its little Plaza. The valley is fertile and cultivated, and is beautiful apart from its picturesque situation. It is dotted with bright, green

View of Caracas from Harper's New Monthly Magazine, *1858. Wood engraving.*

THE CATHEDRAL.

fields of cane and molojo; interspersed with coffee plantations, whose snow-flake blossoms and dark green foliage contrast prettily with the red flowered bucarre tree which shades them, with here a ruin caused by the earthquake, and there the white chimney and buildings of a sugar-mill in the midst of a cane patch. Clusters of houses, lines of straight, tapering willows... light streams milling through the valley, and, to remind one that we are in a tropical climate, tall palm trees scattered over the plain, paths dotted with strings of donkeys stretching over the neighbouring heights, the contrast between the rough, scarred mountains and the rich vegetation in the valley they wall in—all serve to produce a peculiarly pleasing and picturesque effect." It is hardly surprising that distant views of Caracas nestling in the valley of Chacao should have formed the subject of paintings and drawings by Melbye and Pissarro. As these written accounts suggest, the views were eminently picturesque.

Melbye and Pissarro also spent a great deal of their time making excursions to those areas surrounding Caracas. The floor of the valley, the ravines, the small villages, the wooded parts at the foot of the Avila range, the streams and the cascades, the mountain slopes, all come within their compass and are surely more faithfully recorded in Pissarro's less formal drawings. These same sites proved to be popular with later travellers and as Humboldt had earlier declared: "Nowhere perhaps can be found collected together, in so small a space of ground, productions so beautiful, and so remarkable in regard to the geography of plants." It is notable that Pissarro in particular as an artist responded to his tropical surroundings with equal enthusiasm, expressed above all in a group of watercolours of the forests and the plants. "Nothing," writes Humboldt as though in defence of Pissarro, "can be more picturesque in a climate, where so many plants have broad, large, shining, and corraceous leaves, than the aspect of trees at a great depth, and illumined by the almost perpendicular rays of the sun."

Melbye and Pissarro set up a studio in Caracas and seem to have survived on the basis of their paintings. A monochrome wash drawing of their studio reveals that their living was derived from the production of por-

The Artists' Studio, 1854.
Brown wash over pencil.

14

traits and topographical views executed for a local clientele. The city of Caracas, according to Chesterton, had "four or five streets of about a mile and a quarter in length, running parallel to each other, which are intersected by others... The houses (as in all South American towns) are whitewashed outside, and some of them tastefully ornamented with carving work and paintings: they do not exceed one story, as, owing to the frequency of earthquakes, much danger would attend their being built higher: but the space each house occupies below makes amends for the deficiency in height... The trade of Caracas is very considerable, as persons from other towns and distant parts come there for the purchase of goods. The shops make a good display in many streets, and there is a constant ingress and egress of mules, laden either with produce for embarkation, or with imported goods for internal consumption... The streets of this city are wide and well paved, and everything has an air of great neatness." Even so the devastation caused by the major earthquake of 1812 was everywhere apparent and can be seen in the drawings made by Sir Robert Ker Porter. A sketching tablet, supplied by the English firm of Ackermann and Co. used by Pissarro in Caracas in 1853-1854, is fortunately still intact. It has several sheets with studies of figures observed in the market places, streets and houses of Caracas, as though bearing out Chesterton's description.

The artists seem to have experienced little difficulty in settling in Caracas. Sympathy for their surroundings was enhanced by the cultural opportunities presented by the city and by the company of several fellow artists. Humboldt observed that "Civilization has in no other part of South America assumed a more European physiognomy." He found at Caracas "in several families a taste for instruction, a knowledge of the masterpieces of French and Italian literature, and a particular predilection for music, which is cultivated with success." On the other hand, "The mathematical sciences, drawing, painting, cannot here boast of any of those establishments, with which royal munificence, and the patriotic zeal of the inhabitants have enriched Mexico." Melbye's subsequent friendship and collaboration with Ramon Paez, the son of General José Antonio Paez,

Fritz Melbye (1826-1896). View of Caracas. Pencil.

View of Caracas. Pencil.

who was educated in England and spent a great deal of time in exile in New York, underscores the cultural cross-currents that were at work in Caracas in the mid-nineteenth century. Again scenes of cultural life in the city were captured by Pissarro in drawings, although he much preferred studying the landscape and the peasant population. Melbye, in contrast with Pissarro, showed little interest in genre scenes.

The visit to Venezuela with Fritz Melbye presented Pissarro with an opportunity to increase his technical

Three Sheets of Studies from a Sketchbook, 1852-1854.
Pen and ink over pencil.

facility and to broaden his interests. Under Melbye's tutelage there is a noticeable improvement in the technical sophistication of the drawings in all media. Many of these sheets are compositional and were clearly intended as the basis for paintings. Whether these were actually brought to fruition cannot be ascertained now, but it does seem as though Pissarro followed Melbye's traditional working methods, proceeding carefully stage by stage, perfecting detail and compositional balance, through the preparatory drawings to the final painting, as adumbrated by any academy at this date. Pissarro, however, continued to make numerous studies on sheets forming part of large sketching tablets used over a long period and positively teeming with figure and landscape studies many of which were not developed any further. It was by such means that Pissarro was all this time building up his visual repertoire, tentatively exploring motifs that were to recur throughout the rest of his œuvre.

Pissarro's Venezuelan drawings reveal a greater confidence in the handling of media. The pen is used more freely, but it is with the pencil that Pissarro achieves a wider variety in application. Following Melbye's example, Pissarro adopts accented lines and carefully controlled hatching, turning the pencil onto its side and varying the tonal value for different parts of the composition. The handling of watercolour, however, is a revelation. Whether used on small or large scale, there is a remarkable aplomb in the treatment of this difficult medium. There is great variety in the use of watercolour for topographical views and genre scenes made in Caracas, or the surrounding districts, leading to the abandon characterizing the studies of tropical vegetation where the washes overpower the skeletal framework lightly sketched beneath in pencil. Where Humboldt for the illustrations accompanying his botanical publications tempered his enthusiasm as a true scientist, Pissarro's response is predominantly expansive and unrestricted.

Although the best known of Pissarro's paintings of South American subjects were undertaken after 1855, it is, nonetheless, possible to draw some conclusions about his work as a whole. Both the numerous drawings and the few surviving paintings share a com-

Bridge of Doña Romualda, 1854. Watercolour over pencil.

positional assurance that is exceptional in a young artist. Pissarro seems from the first, almost innately, to have had no difficulty in organizing the spatial divisions within a composition. He retained this intrinsic ability throughout his life, but there can be no doubt that it was evolved rapidly at the outset as much by Melbye's help as by the need to reduce the chaotic effulgence of tropical vegetation to some sense of order. This is surely the meaning behind Cézanne's comment made in conversation with Joachim Gasquet: "Pissarro had the good luck to be born in the Antilles. There he learned to draw without masters."

A painting like *Coconut Palms by the Sea, St. Thomas* (1856) shows how well Pissarro could apply the lessons absorbed in South America. The play of the vertical against the horizontal in the foreground, offset by the diagonal created by the receding shore line in the middle distance, is exemplary. So, too, is the progression from foreground to background aided by the pathway along which two small figures move and by the silhouetting of the coconut palms against the expanse of sky. The palette is restricted mainly to browns and yellows, but Pissarro supplies accents of colour on the figures to enliven the uncluttered composition. All these devices helped to create a feeling of unity and they were to become standard procedure in Pissarro's mature works.

A great deal of attention has been paid to Camille Pissarro's work and ambience before he settled permanently in France in 1855 because it can be too easily overlooked. He arrived in Paris aged twenty-five as a developed artist. Neither St. Thomas nor Caracas were totally cut off from European influence. There was, in addition, the discipline exerted by Fritz Melbye, whose experience and technical ability provided a timely sense of direction for Pissarro's work. Beyond Melbye's personal example, there was the fact that, albeit unconsciously, he was a link with two important strands of art. The first, as hinted above, was the European academic tradition through Anton Melbye's training in Copenhagen with Eckersberg. The influential Düsseldorf school, whose practices may have been known to the Melbye brothers, had quite independently established a close and widely acknowledged relationship

Oswald Achenbach (1827-1905). Landscape in the Campagna.

Frederick Edwin Church (1826-1900). The Heart of the Andes, 1859.

with American painters, but Pissarro's knowledge of the north European academic tradition was gleaned indirectly. An affinity can be seen, for example, between Pissarro's *Two Women conversing on the Seashore, St. Thomas* (1856) and *Landscape in the Campagna* (1850-1855) by the Düsseldorf painter Oswald Achenbach. The figures placed prominently in the foreground and seen against a landscape composed of judiciously exploited diagonals, horizontals and gestures are features common to both paintings, although there are important differences in technique arising from age, training and experience. Whatever insistence Melbye may have placed on accepted methods, Pissarro does seem at the outset to have followed and even surpassed his precepts as regards painting, whereas the individual

Two Women conversing on the Seashore, St. Thomas, 1856.

qualities of Pissarro as a burgeoning artist are best represented in the drawings.

The second link that Melbye provided is with those artists who went in search of nature in its primitive state. Thomas Cole and Frederick Edwin Church are famous examples of painters who found in the American landscape an inspirational force of this kind. It is not that Melbye had any personal contact with either of these artists (none is recorded, although Church did acquire some of Melbye's drawings), but that they all traveled in North and South America deliberately seeking out the sublimity and drama of nature. Pissarro's own reactions are reflected in the spontaneity of his vivid watercolours. He did not, however, distil these reactions into finished paintings, like Cole and Church, and he did not at this stage of his life appreciate any symbolical or allegorical significance in nature. Rather, Pissarro's response may be likened to Thomas Cole's reaction on visiting the Catskill Mountains in 1835: "The painter of American scenery has, indeed, privileges superior to any other. All nature here is new to art. No Tivolis, Ternis, Mont Blancs, Plinlimmons, hack-

neyed and worn by the daily pencils of hundreds; but primeval forests, virgin lakes, and waterfalls, feasting his eye with new delights, and filling his portfolio with their features of beauty and magnificence, hallowed to his soul by their freshness from the creation, for his own favoured pencil."

Camille Pissarro must have carried these images of nature as seen in St. Thomas and Venezuela with him to France in 1855 and it is worth pondering whether he ever recounted his memories to Paul Gauguin when they met towards the end of the 1870s. Certainly Pissarro reached Paris with his interest in landscape and peasant life already aroused—the two subjects which he was later to develop at length. This visual curiosity was matched by a technical assurance achieved essentially by his own efforts and only with a little guidance or prompting from Melbye. Add to this the advantage of seeing landscape under the intense light of the tropical zone and one can appreciate how Pissarro arrived in Paris as a nascent Impressionist painter. He was, as one recent writer has expressed it, "born into a state of 'impressionism'."

La Varenne-Saint-Hilaire, View from Champigny, c. 1863.

Interior of the Palais des Beaux-Arts,
Universal Exhibition, Paris, 1855.
From The Illustrated London News,
1 September 1855.

Arrival in France

CAMILLE PISSARRO was no stranger to Paris. While at school at Passy between 1841-1847 he apparently spent his holidays in Paris with relatives and by the time he arrived in the city in November 1855 his mother was already established there. The years immediately following Pissarro's arrival were critical, for he was faced with the task of measuring the progress made in St. Thomas and Venezuela against the full range of French art that he could now examine more circumspectly. His family provided him with some financial assistance, but the situation was complicated by the fact that Pissarro was not keen to mould himself after successful Salon painters, or even the two Melbye brothers, and by the fact that he formed a liaison with his mother's maid, Julie Vellay, whom he did not marry until 1871 after the birth of two of their children. Such factors caused distress to this essentially middle-class family and Pissarro's frustrations at this time are perhaps expressed in his comments made later

about Armand Guillaumin in a letter of 1878 written to Eugène Murer: "I was at St. Thomas in 1852 in a well paid job, but I couldn't stick it. Without more ado I cut the whole thing and bolted to Caracas in order to get clear of the bondage of bourgeois life. What I have been through you can't imagine, and what I am still suffering is terrible, very much more than when young and full of enthusiasm and ardour, convinced as I now am that I have no future to look forward to. Nevertheless it seems to me that, if I had to begin over again, I should do precisely the same thing. Does that mean that one ought to advise a friend to go and do likewise? It all depends on the temperament, the convictions of the individual."

Pissarro was a man of particularly strong convictions. His single aim as an artist was to be as faithful as possible to those sensations he experienced before nature. In the application of this principle Pissarro was unwavering and it was as much his conscious pursuit of

*Photograph of paintings by Ingres
at the Universal Exhibition, Paris, 1855.*

*Photograph of the Grand Salon Carré,
Universal Exhibition, Paris, 1855.*

it as the display of any technical skills that resulted in the artist's immense influence on painters of different generations. During a period of great artistic fecundity in the second half of the nineteenth century in France Pissarro remained a constant, able to come to terms with originality and quick to detect hypocrisy of any kind. It is apparent that he already possessed these attributes at the age of twenty-five when he arrived in France to be confronted by the Universal Exhibition of 1855. There are admittedly moments of indecision shortly after Pissarro's arrival as to the type of painter he would become, but the technical ability and compositional assurance detected in his work before 1855 are retained. The large canvases exhibited in the annual Salons towards the close of the 1860s are among the most remarkable landscapes of the nineteenth century carrying within them the seeds of future developments in European painting from whence issued not only Impressionism, but also certain aspects of Post-Impressionism. The present chapter attempts to analyse Pissarro's reactions to his first sustained examination of French art and to trace his development through the transitional years of the 1850s and 1860s.

The Universal Exhibition in Paris (May–November, 1855) was intended to surpass the Great Exhibition of 1851 held in London at the Crystal Palace. Interestingly, Pissarro saw the Crystal Palace for himself when he fled to England in 1870 to escape the Franco-Prussian war. The exhibition in Paris was the largest and most ambitious ever held at that date. It was mounted by Napoleon III basically as a political exercise to restore self-confidence in France. Housed in huge structures of metal and glass erected along the side of the Avenue des Champs-Elysées and the Avenue Montaigne, the Palais de l'Industrie was a shrine to technological and industrial progress, serving "to entertain the public and to enhance a prevailing sense of easy optimism among an increasingly powerful bourgeoisie." Where the Universal Exhibition of 1855 surpassed the Great Exhibition of 1851 was in the representation of the arts. Over 5,000 works were divided between three large halls in a separate building (Palais des Beaux-Arts) with space for twenty-nine participating nations. Chief among these was France in an attempt to reaffirm the international prestige of French culture. Well over half the works in the exhibition were by French artists and the opportunity was taken to instal retrospective displays of Ingres, Delacroix, Horace Vernet and Alexandre Decamps. In addition to paintings, there were watercolours and prints on the upper floor. Altogether the section devoted to the arts was not a success. The public was more interested in scientific and technological items and the attendance was poor even after a reduction in the price of tickets. Critics were overwhelmed by the indigestible size of the displays, and, like Baudelaire, were forced in the circumstances to concentrate on the works of Ingres and Delacroix. In short, the selection was too large and the quality too varied.

For Pissarro, however, the Universal Exhibition was a timely reminder of his artistic heritage. Although, as one writer has expressed it, the "very retrospective and official character of the exhibition tended to restrict its value as an index of contemporary accomplishment," Pissarro had been starved of opportunities such as this. Some of the paintings he might conceivably have known in reproduction, but now he could consult several masterpieces by Ingres and Delacroix in the original, as well as numerous works by artists as varied as Couture, Chassériau, Heim, Meissonier, Cabanel, Gérôme and Bouguereau. These artists represented the taste of the general public of the Second Empire condemned by the critic Edmond Duranty in his short-lived periodical *Réalisme* as "visions of Greece, visions of Rome, medieval visions, visions of the sixteenth, seventeenth and eighteenth centuries," quite divorced from everyday life. Yet, Pissarro could hardly have failed to notice that across the Avenue Montaigne there was a separate pavilion specially installed by Gustave Courbet for those of his pictures that had been refused by the organizers of the main exhibition. Here he displayed *A Burial at Ornans, The Studio* and *The Return from the Fair* amongst a total of forty works, a gesture which, according to Baudelaire, had "all the violence of an armed revolt." The contrast between the Grand Salon Carré in the main part of the Universal Exhibition and Courbet's pavilion (Pavillon du Réalisme) was indicative of the forces at work within French painting at the time. For younger painters, who were refused access to the Salon, or who could not satisfy the authorities of the official Académie des Beaux-Arts, Courbet's defiance was an important lead, encouraging dissident groups to show their own work away from the Salon. Thus the realist painter François Bonvin used

his own studio in 1859 to display paintings by those rejected from the Salon of that year. Similarly, Courbet in 1867 repeated his gesture of 1855 by again housing his own paintings in a separate pavilion, being imitated on this occasion by Manet. Such acts of independence, as well as the Salon des Refusés of 1863 in which Pissarro exhibited three works, served as prototypes for the Impressionist exhibitions held between 1874 and 1886, and for the Salon des Indépendants associated with Neo-Impressionism.

Understandably, in this state of flux Pissarro kept an open mind about the direction in which he would develop his art after 1855. His paintings and drawings attest his interest in different strands of art, but there were, in addition, other more general factors symbolized by the Universal Exhibition that helped to determine the character of Camille Pissarro's work; namely, the importance of drawing and the need to honour artistic tradition. Armed with a letter of recommendation to the artist Henri Lehmann, an influential teacher at the Ecole des Beaux-Arts, Pissarro enrolled in private classes given by other official teachers at the Ecole, such as François-Edouard Picot and Isidore Dagnan. Several sheets of academic studies made from posed models

Gustave Courbet (1819-1877). Peasants of Flagey returning from the Fair, 1851.

might have been drawn at these private classes, or, alternatively, at the Académie Suisse, an informal studio run by a former artists' model, Père Suisse, on the corner of Boulevard du Palais and Quai des Orfèvres where Pissarro met many of his future colleagues in the Impressionist movement. Pissarro's drawings are reminiscent of those executed by Cézanne at similar sessions. At the same time Pissarro was making careful compositional drawings of landscapes during the 1860s, as though plotting the landscape like a cartographer. So far no drawings after model books have been found and there is only one very slight study after classical statuary. It is, therefore, hardly possible to describe Pissarro as following the tenets of academic drawing slavishly, yet his adherence to the importance of drawing, which he maintained throughout his life, can be seen as an acknowledgement of academic discipline. On the whole, Pissarro's attitude to drawing at this early stage of his life is perhaps closer to the alternative methods promulgated by Horace Lecoq de Boisbaudran, whose *L'Education de la mémoire pittoresque* (1848) achieved widespread popularity and was upheld by the important reforms of 1863 when official responsibility for art schools in France was wrested from the Académie des Beaux-Arts and placed in the hands of a more open-minded and politically conscious government. A teacher at the Ecole Royale et Spéciale de Dessin, Lecoq devised a series of exercises intended to develop the powers of visual memory and observation. One of his exercises was to ask students to make drawings from moving models; another was to encourage students to sketch out-of-doors, as opposed to working with a single source of light in the studio. The purpose was to express the "essential spirit" of a subject instead of its literal aspects.

An echo of these methods, as well as Pissarro's own wide experience of drawing, can be found in the artist's letters to his eldest son, Lucien. On 13 June 1883 Pissarro writes: "Degas says that there is one way of escaping Legros' influence, the method is simply this: it is to reproduce, in your own place, from memory the drawing you make in class… You will have your difficulties, but a moment will come when you will be astonished by the ease with which you retain forms,

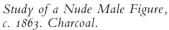

Study of a Nude Male Figure,
c. 1863. Charcoal.

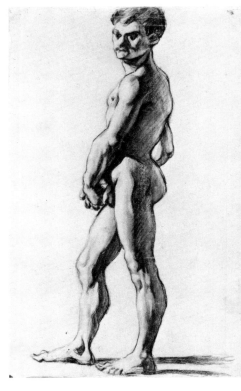

Paul Cézanne (1839-1906).
Study of a Nude Male Figure. Charcoal.

and, curiously enough, the observations you make from memory will have far more power and be much more original than those you owe to direct contact with nature." Again in July 1883 he advised Lucien: "It is good to draw everything, anything… When you have trained yourself to see a tree truly, you know how to look at the human figure." The discipline of drawing, inculcated while in St. Thomas and Venezuela, was not lost after Pissarro's arrival in France and it remained a firm basis for his art. Only Degas amongst the Impressionists drew as consistently as Pissarro and prepared his compositions on paper with as much care. For both artists, however, drawing played a more important role than just the preparation of paintings or prints. Pissarro spent a great deal of time recording images and figures seen in real life simply to re-use them later, his sketchbooks being a means of building up a visual repertoire. Only during the 1880s when he became more interested in the human figure and during the 1890s when he was less mobile did Pissarro again draw from posed models. The chief importance of drawing for Pissarro, however, lay in the fact that it was a way of recording images spontaneously. For him the overriding task of the Impressionist painter was to recapture that spontaneity on the canvas, and drawings were the best means for the transmission of the artist's initial reactions to a motif. In short, Pissarro is an Impressionist artist who felt compelled to draw as much as to paint, or to make prints, and this desire goes some way to repudiate the traditional concept of Impressionist painting as the product of a single spontaneous act.

Pissarro's first experiences in France both confirmed the validity of the methods adopted in the Antilles and encouraged him to modify them. As a draughtsman, therefore, he experimented a great deal during these years varying the media and using coloured papers. A portrait of Julie Vellay's niece can resemble similar sheets by Degas influenced by Ingres, whereas a study of Julie Vellay herself nursing Lucien Pissarro evokes comparison with Fantin-Latour both in the treatment of subject and technique. Landscape drawings, usually on pale blue, grey or light brown paper are often in mixed media with outlines in pencil and hatching in pen

François Bonvin (1817-1887). Woman Ironing, 1858.

Portrait of Julie Vellay's Niece Marie Daudon. Pencil.

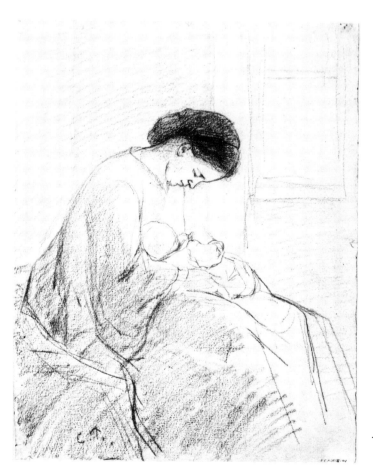

Julie Vellay nursing Lucien, 1865. Charcoal.

Study of a Tree at Chailly. Charcoal.

and ink, or also heightened with a wash. But here, too, as in Corot, there is a contrast between fine pencil line and broadly drawn strokes in charcoal or chalk highlighted with white. It is an impressive range revealing Pissarro's adaptability and technical skill, notably in the delicacy with which he could apply the softer media.

On 16 April 1860 Pissarro registered as a copyist in the Musée du Louvre, but he does not seem to have taken advantage of this facility. Where Manet, Degas and Cézanne made numerous direct copies after old masters, either from the original or from prints, none by Pissarro has survived. Nevertheless, the Universal Exhibition did impose on him a sense of historical perspective that became a vital part of his artistic character. On several occasions in his letters Pissarro discusses the antecedents for Impressionism, particularly with regard to the future publication of a book by an Englishman, Wynford Dewhurst, entitled *Impressionist Painting: Its Genesis and Development*. First issued as a series of articles in *The Studio* in 1903, the book was published in 1904. In it Dewhurst quotes a letter that the painter had written at the author's request in November 1902 regarding Pissarro's visit to England in 1870: "In 1870 I found myself in London with Monet, and we met Daubigny and Bonvin. Monet and I were very enthusiastic over London landscapes… We also visited the museums. The water colours and paintings of Turner and Constable, the canvases of Old Crome have certainly had an influence on us. We admired Gainsborough, Lawrence, Reynolds, etc., but we were struck chiefly by the landscape painters who shared more in our aim with regard to plein-air, light and fugitive effects. Watts, Rossetti strongly interested us amongst the modern men." Yet, when commenting on Dewhurst's text Pissarro wrote in a letter (8 May 1903) to Lucien: "He [Dewhurst] omits the influence which Claude Lorrain, Corot, the whole eighteenth century and Chardin especially exerted on us." He apparently reiterated this point in a further letter to Dewhurst: "I do not think, as you say, that the Impressionists are connected with the English School, for many reasons too long to develop here. It is true that Turner and Constable have been useful to us, as all painters of great talent have; but the base of our art is evidently of French tradition, our masters are Clouet, Nicolas Poussin, Claude Lorrain, the eighteenth century with Chardin, and 1830 with Corot."

The first chapter of Dewhurst's book, conceivably prompted by Pissarro's letter of 1902, argued that the origins of Impressionist painting could be traced to British painting. In fact, Pissarro's interest in earlier periods of art extended further than the French and English schools. Following the example of realist painters like François Bonvin and of Barbizon painters like Théodore Rousseau he also closely examined the works of Dutch seventeenth-century genre and landscape artists. Some specific visual sources for Pissarro's work will be mentioned later on, but it is important to realize that the painter examined a whole range of art. "When you have occasion to," he wrote to Lucien in 1883, "look at the Persians, the Chinese, the Japanese. Derive your taste from these who are truly strong, for you must always go to the source: in painting to the primitives, in sculpture to the Egyptians, in miniature to the Persians, etc., etc." A further letter to Lucien, this time written in Rouen in 1896, reports: "I have just come from the library. I have been looking at illuminated books. Flemish works of the thirteenth century and Gothic French of the fourteenth and fifteenth centuries, admirable books, some in the bindings of the time and very beautiful."

Now, this fascination for a diversity of styles was clearly nurtured after Pissarro's arrival in France on the basis of the holdings in French museums. Later Pissarro was able to supplement his knowledge with visits to English, Belgian and Dutch museums. What is of particular importance, however, is the way in which Pissarro's knowledge was incorporated into his own work. Unlike Manet, who often quoted visual sources literally, and unlike Degas, who sublimated his knowledge of the history of art by oblique references, Pissarro tended to view earlier periods of art in a far more empirical way. Just as there are no direct copies after old masters in Pissarro's painted œuvre, only a single drawing can be so claimed, and that is after the portrait *La belle Zélie* by Ingres in the Musée des Beaux-Arts at Rouen. Pissarro's attitude to the past is, therefore, somewhat ambivalent: his interest in it is clearly documented, yet in his work it is almost deliberately concealed. The explanation for this is again provided by a statement made in one of the letters to Lucien. "If we were to borrow hands or feet from Dürer, I think the result would not be satisfactory... We Impressionists have precisely the opposite attitude... we have an altogether different concept of what it means to be inspired by the ancients. We ask nothing better than to be classics, but we want to achieve that in terms of our own experience; how different that is!" (26 November 1896).

The famous letter written by Cézanne to his son, Paul, in 1906 refers to a specific case of someone slavishly borrowing from the old masters. "We are agreed on this point, that he [Emile Bernard] is an intellectual, constipated by recollections of museums, but who does not look enough at nature, and that is the great thing, to make himself free from the school and indeed from all schools. So that Pissarro was not mistaken, though he went a little too far, when he said that all the necropoles of art should be burned down." It is apparent in this context that Pissarro was not objecting so much to the contents of museums as to the way in which they were used. For himself and for his fellow Impressionists their attitude to the past was more a question of the expression of their own individuality through the past than one of imitation. As Pissarro wrote to Lucien in March 1898, "The real question is *personality, individuality*. Nobody would think of denying the strongly marked individuality of a Rembrandt, or even of a Manet, who

Théodore Rousseau (1812-1867). The Village of Becquigny.

comes from Goya but brings an entirely different vision, a very specific and modern consciousness, which Goya could not have envisaged. That Corot comes from Claude Lorrain and reflects him is evident, but it is also clear to what degree he transformed what he took, in this lies all his genius: his figures are as modern as you please. In short, it is only here [in France] that artists are faithful to the tradition of the great masters *without robbing them*." The radicalism of Impressionism, therefore, was not that it broke with the past, but, rather, the uses to which it was prepared to put the art of previous centuries.

Although a lifelong admirer of Ingres and Delacroix, the artists to whom Camille Pissarro was perhaps instinctively drawn at the Universal Exhibition were those associated with the Barbizon school and the forest of Fontainebleau—Corot, Daubigny, Théodore Rousseau, Millet, Diaz and Troyon. Pissarro maintained close contact with Danish artists, working for a time as an assistant for Anton Melbye (apparently completing the sky in some of Melbye's paintings) and sharing a studio with David Jacobsen. While declaring himself a pupil of Anton Melbye for his Salon entries in 1859 and 1866, for those in 1864 and 1865 he described himself as a pupil jointly of Melbye and Corot; whereas, for the Salons of 1868, 1869 and 1870, the artist admits no allegiance, presumably as an indication of his maturity. Yet, Pissarro's early mature style in France, attained by the mid-1860s, amounts to an amalgam of Corot, Daubigny and Courbet. Of these artists, Corot's example seems to have been the first in the ascendant. He was a painter with whom Pissarro had a special affinity and the younger artist was proud enough of the association to own two drawings by the master now in New York and Oxford respectively. Corot's sympathy for nature ("Go into the country. The muse is in the woods") and his stress on tonal values were obvious points of contact between the two men. Monet records that Corot told Pissarro, "Since you are an artist, you don't need advice. Except for this: above all one must study values. We don't see in the same way: you see green and I see grey and blond! But that is no reason for you not to work at values, for they are the basis and the background of painting. In whatever way one may feel and express oneself, one cannot do good painting without them." Pissarro followed Corot's example and, sometimes in the company of the master's other pupils, searched for motifs out of Paris in the rural setting of the Ile de France (Montmorency) and along the banks of the Seine, the Marne and the Oise (La Roche-Guyon, La Varenne-Saint-Maur, Pontoise).

Pissarro's first success at the Salon was in 1859 when a painting of Montmorency was accepted. Unfortunately, the picture is lost, but numerous drawings done in Montmorency in that year reveal an unprecedented concentration of activity in that area searching for a motif. Whether this Salon painting reflects Corot's style or not cannot be established now. Pissarro was capable of painting in more than one style in a single year, so that while *Corner of a Village* (1863) with its dabs of colour and accumulation of detail evokes comparison with a realist painter such as Adolphe Hervier, a landscape, *La Varenne-Saint-Hilaire, View from Champigny* (1863), is clearly dependent upon the painters of the Barbizon school. The supple brushwork used for the trees, the light filtering across from the right, the treatment of the lengthening shadows and the field with the wide expanse of blue sky above, all emulate Corot. On the other hand, the fussier manner used for rendering the grass and the foliage is more reminiscent of Daubigny or Rousseau. The culmination of Pissarro's interest in Corot's technique is perhaps found in *The Towpath*, exhibited in the Salon of 1864. An oil sketch for this painting exists, proving that Pissarro

was still using traditional methods for the preparation of important large-scale paintings. The differences between the oil sketch and the finished painting are considerable. Like another oil sketch dating from this period, *The Ferry at La Varenne-Saint-Hilaire*, the style is lively and the palette varied. The brushstrokes are small and hurried, as in the treatment of the clouds. The finished painting of *The Towpath*, however, is far more rigid. Nearly all of the principal features are retained, but they have been more firmly anchored and the palette has darkened and become more unified. Almost reflectively, Pissarro has placed himself further away from the scene in the finished painting, as though to diminish the pivotal role that the advancing figure has in the geometry of the composition. There can be little doubt that the oil sketch is the more accurate representation of the scene and that the simplification necessitated for the creation of the final painting results in a compromise. It was this type of falsification that Impressionist painters were determined to eliminate.

The subject of *The Towpath* is one that can be found just as easily in Daubigny's œuvre as in Corot's. Indeed, *The Banks of the Marne at Chennevières*, which was exhibited in the Salon of 1865, is a riverscape that might have been directly inspired by Daubigny. Chennevières lies on a hill opposite La Varenne-Saint-Hilaire on the banks of the Marne, where Pissarro had first painted in 1863 and lived for part of 1864. The composition is conceived as a panoramic view; the river with its profusion of reeds and weed in the foreground, a short curving bank on the left, a long, gently descending slope on the right, and the sky above. The wide expanse

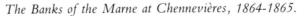
The Banks of the Marne at Chennevières, 1864-1865.

The Ferry at La Varenne-Saint-Hilaire, 1864.

of sky and river, one reflected in the other, strikes a balance, while the main features emphasizing the bend in the river are placed in the middle of the composition. The only hint of human activity is restricted to the boat crossing the river just to left of centre. The blue parasol held by one of the figures in the boat suggests that it is summer. Another possible indication of human activity lies in the white mill, or factory, placed centrally and marking the exact point where the diagonals, extending from the corners of the composition, cross. The building implies a specific economic activity in a landscape that might otherwise be mistaken for a timeless image of rural leisure. This is a dichotomy that frequently occurs in Pissarro's work in the next decade. Another feature of this painting that became a hallmark of the painter's style before the end of the 1860s is the treatment of the architectural elements. The brown and salmon-pink roofs of the buildings, together with the white walls, offset the predominant tones of blue and green. The forms of the buildings are prescribed by the sunlight, which, as indicated by the parasol held by the figure in the boat, comes from the right. The sides of the buildings in direct sunlight are depicted in pure white, while those in shadow lack the same degree of luminosity. From the first, Pissarro was an extremely articulate painter.

Charles-François Daubigny (1817-1878). River Scene near Bonnières, 1857.

The Banks of the Marne in Winter, 1866.

*Gustave Courbet (1819-1877). Young Ladies of the Village giving
Alms to a Cow Girl in a Valley near Ornans, 1851-1852.*

The Donkey Ride at La Roche-Guyon, c. 1864-1865.

◁ *The Hillsides of L'Hermitage, Pontoise, c. 1867.*

Edgar Degas (1834-1917). The Carriage at the Race Meeting, 1870-1873.

The Banks of the Marne in Winter, exhibited in the Salon of 1866, is notable for its economy. The composition comprises the path along the river and the hillside in the background, leading down to a group of buildings. It is a cloudy, damp, blustery day; the trees are bare. It is a solemn picture, subdued in colouring, elemental in construction and bold in execution. The most surprising aspect is the wedge driven from the lower right corner towards the centre of the painting. This open ground is balanced on the left in the upper half of the composition by the hillside, but clamping these two complementary parts together are the buildings on the right, characterized by tall bare walls and steep gables. The audacity of leaving a large area such as this blank in the foreground of a picture was noted by the novelist and art critic Emile Zola, who in his review of this Salon commented on Pissarro's style: "You should realize that you will please no one, and that your picture will be found too bare, too bleak. Then why the devil do you have the arrogant clumsiness to paint solidly and to study nature frankly... An austere and serious kind of painting, an extreme concern for truth and accuracy, a rugged and strong will. You are a great blunderer, sir—you are an artist that I like."

A much smaller painting that shows a less dramatic, but, nevertheless, daring use of space is *The Donkey Ride at La Roche-Guyon* dating from the mid-1860s. Pissarro has painted two middle-class women and a boy taking it in turns to ride on the donkeys provided by two peasant children. Compositionally, the painting takes its cue from Gustave Courbet's *Young Ladies of the Village giving Alms to a Cow Girl in a Valley near Ornans*, which Pissarro could have seen when it was exhibited in 1855. Both paintings are open to political interpretation, but in containing his figures in a wide open field, extending far away into the distance with the figures close to the front plane of the picture, Pissarro telescopes space in a way that anticipates Degas' paintings of the 1870s. The radicalism of this small picture is almost denied by the beauty of the Corotesque landscape with La Roche-Guyon in the background on the left and a steamer making its way down river on the right. It is a landscape that the painter explored thoroughly during the 1860s.

Pissarro's style reaches full maturity with a series of magisterial paintings undertaken for exhibition at the Salon during the final years of the 1860s and displayed there at the instigation of Daubigny. *La Côte du Jallais, Pontoise*, *The Hillsides of L'Hermitage, Pontoise*, *The Hermitage at Pontoise* and *Landscape at Les Pâtis, Pontoise*, are amongst the most forcefully conceived and powerfully executed landscapes of the nineteenth century. One other, *View of L'Hermitage, Pontoise*, also belongs to this category, but its present whereabouts is unknown.

These canvases, painted with broad brushes, are the result of a concentrated examination of the semi-rural area of Pontoise known as L'Hermitage where Pissarro lived between 1866-1868. Each work explores the spatial tensions between the landscape and the buildings. Pissarro makes skilful use of the terrain, so that in *La Côte du Jallais*, *The Hillsides of L'Hermitage* and *Landscape at Les Pâtis* a pathway leads the eye into the valley below where the houses and the trees lead the eye upwards again to the top of the hillside. Natural features are, therefore, compressed and, accordingly, the paint is applied in wide bands, creating a ribbed effect. Each canvas is dependent upon a geometric framework involving verticals, horizontals and diagonals of varying angles. The figures on the curving pathways emphasize the dramatic potential within each picture. As in *The Banks of the Marne in Winter*, it is the architectural elements that serve to lock the various parts of the painting together, so that it is the buildings that anchor and pivot the composition. Zola particularly admired *La Côte du Jallais* and something of its impact can be detected in his terse description of the painting. "A valley, a few houses with their roofs seen on the level of a bare climbing path; then, on the other side, in the background, a cultivated hillside divided into strips of green and brown. This is truly a modern countryside. One feels that man has passed through it turning the soil and harrowing it, delimiting the horizons. This valley and hillside have a simplicity, an heroic frankness. Nothing would be so banal if it was not so all-encompassing. The painter's insight has wrested from daily truth a rare poem of life and strength."

In these paintings Pissarro explores on a large scale the full potential of a type of landscape essayed by Corot as early as the 1820s and 1830s. In *Ville-d'Avray, the Pond and the Cabassud House*, for instance, there is also a foreground that descends into a valley where houses are seen against a distant hillside. In the painting by Corot, however, the light tends to be distributed evenly over the buildings, whereas Pissarro uses light to define shapes and forms, thereby activating the surface. Baudelaire referred in his review of the 1859 Salon to Corot's "deep feeling for constructing" and described him as an artist who "observes the proportional value of each detail within the whole".

While the compositions of *La Côte du Jallais*, *The Hillsides of L'Hermitage* and *Landscape at Les Pâtis* could be described as enlargements of works by Corot, the palette and brushwork owes more to Courbet. There is a great variety of brushstroke within each of these paintings. The influence of Corot still lingers in the treatment of the tall pencil-shaped poplar trees, but the broader application of paint and the tendency to overlay paint surfaces is closer to Courbet's technique, as is the palette dominated by green, brown and cream white. The strength of Pissarro's brushwork in these paintings is comparable with that found in the early paintings of Manet and Monet.

The Hermitage at Pontoise (1867) is a different composition from those just discussed. It depends principally upon the horizontal, with the result that the composition is read in strips upwards—the *jardin potager* in the foreground, the houses in the middle distance nestling against the hillside, and the sky above studded with grey clouds. The economy of Pissarro's handling becomes apparent if the painting is compared with Daubigny's *View of Butry near Valmondois*, dating from 1866 and on a comparable scale, which could have served as Pissarro's starting point. Daubigny's painting appears confused; the relationships between the various parts are obfuscated; the eye distracted by anecdotal detail and the over-elaborate brushwork. The strength of Pissarro's painting is best seen in the treatment of the houses and their reticulated walls. Detailed examination reveals how the broadest brushes have been used and how, if seen in isolation, these passages stand alone

as individual compositions. Indeed, the roofs and walls of the houses possess the qualities of abstract painting, just as areas of void assume positive shapes. *The Hermitage at Pontoise*, therefore, as well as Pissarro's other Salon pictures of the late 1860s, assume great importance for the developments of French painting and especially for Cézanne, as will be seen in a later chapter.

Significantly, it was Cézanne's boyhood friend, Emile Zola, who was one of the first critics to recognize the virtues of Pissarro's style during the late 1860s. Zola's Salon criticism of 1868 contains eloquent passages on these paintings of L'Hermitage in an attempt to bring Pissarro's work to public notice. They deserve to be quoted at some length: "The artist only cares for the solemn truth: he places himself before a landscape resolved to depict the full grandeur of the horizon without adding the slightest touch of his own invention; he is neither poet nor philosopher, but simply an observer of nature, a recorder of skies and of the earth. You may dream dreams if you want to, but this is what he has seen… The originality is here profoundly human. It is not derived from a certain facility of hand or from a falsification of nature. It stems from the temperament of the painter himself and comprises a feeling for truth resulting from an inner conviction. Never before have paintings appeared to me to possess such an over-

Camille Corot (1796-1875).
Ville-d'Avray, the Pond and the Cabassud House, 1835-1840.

The Hermitage at Pontoise, 1867.

whelming dignity. One can almost hear the inner voices of the earth and sense the trees burgeoning. The boldness of the horizons, the disdain of any show, the complete lack of cheap tricks, imbue the whole with an indescribable feeling of epic grandeur. Such reality is more than a daydream… Camille Pissarro is one of the three or four genuine painters of the day. He has solidity and a breadth of touch, he paints freely, following tradition like the old masters. I have rarely encountered a technique that is so sure. A beautiful painting by this man is the act of an honest man. I cannot think of a better way of describing his talent."

La Côte du Jallais (Jallais Hill), Pontoise, 1867.

Landscape at Les Pâtis, Pontoise, 1868.

Self-Portrait, 1873.

Attributed to Camille Pissarro.
Self-Portrait, facing front.
Self-Portrait, in three-quarters profile.

Camille Pissarro and the Birth of Impressionism

THE FIRST Impressionist exhibition was held in 1874 at 35, boulevard des Capucines in rooms formerly used by the photographer Nadar. The exhibition lasted for one month only (15 April–15 May) and provoked a great deal of puzzlement and even derision on the part of the critics and the general public. There were thirty participants, who had formed themselves into a cooperative with the title *Société anonyme des artistes peintres, sculpteurs et graveurs.* Pissarro played an active role in the formulation of the rules governing the *Société*, in the organization of the subsequent exhibitions held at intervals up until 1886 at various locations, and in the extension of invitations to artists to participate.

All of these undertakings were to prove difficult and even acrimonious, involving tortuous negotiations in which Pissarro proved to be a firm, but essentially conciliatory, arbiter. He was slightly older than the other artists and had an imposing presence together with a quiet determination that commanded respect. He was also, owing to his financial circumstances, an intensely practical man with considerable experience of official bodies and administrative rules, having been involved since 1860 with the *Association des peintres d'histoire et de genre, sculpteurs, graveurs, architectes et dessinateurs.* It is highly characteristic of Pissarro's political outlook that he should have suggested as a model for the grouping of the Impressionist painters the charter governing the cooperative association of bakers at Pontoise, which he had studied in detail. The *Société anonyme* was deliberately organized as a rebuff to the official Salon. It did not involve a jury system and was intended to promote the sales of those artists who agreed to the charter. Although the *Société anonyme* was disbanded after the first exhibition because it did not prove to be profitable, the basic principles it established were maintained for the rest of the Impressionist exhibitions.

Pissarro's *Self-Portrait* of these years is instructive in any evaluation of his role in Impressionism. The disagreement and sometimes bitter wranglings between the principal Impressionists cannot be recounted in detail here, but an examination of Pissarro's *Self-Portrait* helps to explain his authoritative position within the Impressionist movement. The image is of a man with a high domed forehead, balding, but with a long white beard. He was only forty-three, yet he has the appearance of a prematurely aged man. It is possible that Pissarro cultivated this image of himself. Self-portraits dating from before 1855, including the depiction of himself in the studio in Caracas, show a rather dapper man with bushy hair, short beard and trimmed, curled moustache. Two painted self-portraits in Copenhagen, where the head is seen from different angles to the extent that the sitter seems at first to be two separate individuals, show the beginnings of a full beard and have less emphasis on a moustache. If the identification is correct, it is likely that the portrait with the face in front view was painted first, as the self-portrait in three-quarters profile gives greater prominence to the beard. Unfortunately, these two self-portraits are difficult to date, but their provenance suggests that they were, in all probability, painted shortly after 1855 and perhaps given to Anton Melbye. A self-portrait drawing of the 1860s shows the artist with a longer beard and smoking a pipe, thereby revealing that already within that decade Pissarro's image of himself was firmly established. Later self-portraits occur only toward the very end of his life and are comparatively infrequent within his extensive œuvre. The last self-portrait painted in Paris during the final years of his life, for example, forgoes the philosophical air and replaces it with a slightly humorous image derived from the floppy hat with the curling brim and the quizzical expression over the half-rim glasses.

What is particularly revealing is the way in which Pissarro's contemporaries interpreted his appearance and manner. Numerous portraits by friends, members of his own family and admirers of the younger generation do no more than record the familiar personal attributes of the artist, but written comments provide an insight into his character. The critic Edmond Duranty wrote in *L'Artiste* in 1880: "Monsieur Pissarro is the oldest of the old, aged fifty with the head of an apostle, always with a canvas under each arm. What should La Nouvelle-Athènes, the headquarters of the school say? Salute Moses! He carries the Tablets of the Law." George Moore in his *Reminiscences of the Impressionist Painters* (1906) wrote: "The evenings that Pissarro did not come to take his coffee in La Nouvelle-Athènes were very rare indeed. He was there more frequently than Monet or Degas, and when they were there he sat listening, approving of their ideas, joining in the conversation quietly... Pissarro was a wise and appreciative Jew, and he looked like Abraham; his beard was white and he was bald, though at the time he could not have been much more than fifty." Cézanne in 1902 told Jules Borély, "Pissarro was like a father to me: he was a man you turned to for advice, and he was something like *le bon Dieu.*"

This last phrase finds an echo in the recorded comments of the younger generation of artists and writers, who are perhaps best represented by Thadée Natanson, the editor of *La Revue Blanche*, who wrote in an essay entitled "The Apostle Pissarro": "Whether it was because he was infallible, infinitely kind and just—or was it merely his prominent, beaky nose and long white beard?—in any case, everyone who knew him in the nineties thought of him as something like God the Father." The young Matisse, who was one of the last to benefit directly from Pissarro's advice, encapsulated all of these biblical descriptions of the artist in one vivid comparison: "You could not help liking him, he reminded you of one of the prophets on Moses's well at Dijon"—a comparison that Pissarro would have enjoyed, since he much appreciated the frankness of French Gothic sculpture.

These aspects of Pissarro's personality and character, which were established early on in his career, help to account for his wide influence on French painting during the second half of the nineteenth century. Today, his work and letters must serve as the principal testimony to his remarkable individuality, but a conversation piece by Renoir painted in 1876 bears out many of the recorded opinions. Pissarro is seated seen in profile towards the back of the room, barely visible,

Auguste Renoir (1841-1919).
In the Studio at the rue Saint-Georges, 1876.

and yet, no doubt, advancing cogent, forceful and persuasive arguments. As Ambroise Vollard later wrote, "The first thing that struck one in Pissarro was his air of kindness, of delicacy *(finesse)* and at the same time of serenity."

Cézanne apparently told Joachim Gasquet that Pissarro was entitled to be called the first Impressionist, on the technical basis of eliminating black from his palette. To demonstrate that Pissarro was the founder of Impressionist painting is no longer a feasible exercise, since it is a misconception of the way in which Impressionist painting developed. Impressionism was a remarkably diffuse movement and almost evades strict definition. Its antecedents may be detectable, but its adherents are varied, even if only those who exhibited their work in the eight exhibitions are taken into account. The epicentre of Impressionism may have been Paris, but the movement was not essentially an urban one. Furthermore, its birth took place several years before the first group exhibition, which was actually mounted at a time when forces that were to prove divisive were beginning to assert themselves. Finally, the Impressionist movement lacks a manifesto and the principal written sources are the letters between artists, dealers and collectors, as well as critical reaction to the various exhibitions. Even in April 1895 Camille Pissarro could write to his eldest son: "Impressionist art is still too misunderstood to be able to realize a complete synthesis... I remember that, although I was full of ardour, I didn't conceive, even at forty, the deeper side of the movement we followed instinctively. It was in the air!"

Such legerdemain is borne out by the wide range of artists and pictures included in the first Impressionist exhibition, although Pissarro, Monet, Renoir, Sisley and Degas included works that have come to be regarded as quintessentially Impressionist. Where Renoir and Degas displayed paintings that concentrated upon the human figure in their treatment of subject matter, Pissarro, Monet and Sisley submitted a number of landscapes. This prompted one critic, Armand Silvestre, to write: "At first glance, one can hardly tell what differentiates the paintings of M. Monet from those of M. Sisley, and the latter's manner from M. Pissarro's. A little study soon teaches you that M. Monet is the most adroit and daring, M. Sisley the most harmonious and most timid, M. Pissarro, who is basically the inventor of this painting, the most genuine and most naive." Any superficial resemblance that Silvestre observed perhaps stems from the fact that these three artists did together evolve the basic principles of Impressionism in Louveciennes towards the very end of the 1860s. In essence, the first Impressionist exhibition was the summation of advances made in painting on an informal and almost totally independent basis by individual painters of varying backgrounds and with different training. What united them was the desire to depict momentary sensations and the effects of light or atmosphere in terms of colour. As Pissarro himself wrote to Théodore Duret in May 1873 in defence of Monet, "It is a very studied art, based upon observations, and derived from an entirely new feeling. It is poetry through the harmony of pure colour. Monet is a worshipper of true nature." Spontaneity could only be captured, or recreated, as a result of premeditation, in the same way as a famous actor or actress gives a definitive stage performance only after many rehearsals and long acting experience.

If any place deserves approbation as the birthplace of Impressionism, it is not so much Paris as its suburbs or outlying districts where city dwellers sought relaxation at weekends. Argenteuil, Bougival, Louveciennes, Marly were all within easy reach of Paris after the opening of railways. Here, as at the coastal resorts of northern France, such as Le Havre, Parisians of whatever class could walk, picnic, swim or go boating as a change and relief from their everyday existence in the city. By extension, therefore, Impressionism is often quite correctly referred to as an urban art, but it was not necessarily a metropolitan art form. Pissarro, for example, after owning a house for a few years in Louveciennes moved for a long period of residence to Pontoise, a market-town twenty miles north-west of Paris in the Vexin, only in the next decade to move even further into the country to the small village of Eragny-sur-Epte. It is notable that he maintained, for as long as possible, during the 1870s and early 1880s, a studio in Paris, but this was not so much that he could paint there, as a base to show his work to prospective buyers. He could not rely solely upon dealers, even renowned ones like Durand-Ruel, because of the fluctuations of the art market, which, as a capitalist practice, was governed by general financial trends. Pissarro, therefore, even during the final decade while painting his urban views of Paris, remained a stranger in the city. Similarly, the fact that Impressionist painters depicted themes associated with pleasure does not denote that these paintings are about pleasure. Again, as will be demonstrated, for a man who was so central to the Impressionist movement, Pissarro's life and work challenges our basic understanding of it. Yet, at the outset, from 1869-1872, his work, both technically and from the point of view of subject matter, adheres to the traditional interpretation of Impressionism.

A definite stylistic change can be seen in Pissarro's paintings after the group of pictures devoted to L'Hermitage dating from 1867-1868. The format from 1869 is smaller, the brushstrokes become more fragmented, and there is a greater concern to work with pure colours. The range of subject matter increases, too, incorporating motifs observed mostly in Louveciennes, Pontoise and also England, where Pissarro, along with several other French artists, was forced to take refuge during the Franco-Prussian war and the Paris Commune. The palette becomes brighter, the light sharper, and the artist's eye becomes more investigative, examining moving surfaces, such as water and foliage, or luminous surfaces, such as snow and blossom. This greater variety is also apparent in the artist's commitment to portraits and still lifes where textures and tactility assume more importance, just as in landscapes rain and sunlight absorb the artist's attention.

It seems likely that Pissarro moved from Pontoise to Louveciennes in order to paint in the company of Monet, Renoir and Sisley, who were all working in that region. One of Pissarro's chief characteristics as an artist was his sense of place. He analysed a motif or landscape with an intensity that was certainly shared by

Portrait of Jeanne, 1872.

Still Life: Pears in a Basket, 1872.

Spring at Louveciennes, c. 1870.

The Versailles Road, Louveciennes, 1870.

Alfred Sisley (1839-1899). First Snow at Louveciennes, 1870.

Village Street, Louveciennes, 1871.

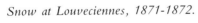

Snow at Louveciennes, 1871-1872.

Alfred Sisley (1839-1899). The Aqueduct at Marly-le-Roi, 1874.

Monet and Sisley, but was perhaps only rivalled by Cézanne. This process of visual dissection is already evident in the canvases of L'Hermitage, but it is also a marked feature of the paintings of Louveciennes and Pontoise. Pissarro did not paint in series like Monet until the 1890s when working in Paris and Rouen on urban themes, but, rather, moved around or looked at the landscape, like a surveyor. Pissarro's method of analysing a motif resulted in the artist distancing himself from it, which has the effect of making his paintings appear remarkably objective. On the other hand, Pissarro's close examination of a motif draws the viewer into it and his predilection for spatial intervals results in the spectator's absorption with the composition. Artist and viewer together both confront the motif and gauge it without actually penetrating it. The chief glory of Pissarro's paintings of the period between the birth of Impressionism and the first Impressionist exhibition is that style and content are perfectly blended. It is, indeed, the moment in Pissarro's working life that people most relish, although it is perhaps not the most significant phase of his art.

Louveciennes is a village only a few miles west of Paris. It overlooks the Seine and lies in close proximity to the Forest and Park of Marly-le-Roi, so called because of its association with the courts of Louis XIV and Louis XV. The transformation of Marly was vividly described by the Duc de Saint-Simon in his *Memoirs*: "In the end, he [Louis XIV] hit on a narrow valley with steep and rocky sides that lay behind Luciennes [Louveciennes]. It was difficult to approach because of the marshes, had no view, was hemmed in by hills on every side, and was exceedingly constricted. On the side of one of the hills was a wretched little hamlet, known as Marly. The fact that this valley was so much enclosed, without any vista or means of making one, was its chief merit in the King's eyes... Gradually, the retreat was enlarged. Piece by piece, the hills were cut away to allow room for building, and a hill at the end of the valley was almost completely levelled so as to give at least one very moderate vista. Finally, with its buildings, fountains, gardens, and aqueducts, so famous, so fascinating under the name of 'La Machine de Marly,' with its forests improved and enclosed, its parklands

and statues, its precious ornaments of all kinds, there arose Marly, as we now see it, although it has been much despoiled since the King's death." Saint-Simon asserts that "It is a modest estimate to say that Versailles, such as we see it, did not cost as much as Marly." His final judgement was that "Marly was typical of the King's bad taste in everything, and of the proud pleasure which he found in subduing Nature, from which diversion neither the most pressing needs of war, nor religious zeal, could ever turn him."

Pissarro, however, gives no hint of the former grandeur of Marly-le-Roi and its region. He skirts the edge of the surrounding forests and only depicts the famous aqueduct, which Sisley painted with dramatic force, in the backgrounds of his pictures. The motifs that absorbed both Pissarro and Sisley were the streets and slopes of Louveciennes, where stolid local inhabitants have supplanted the florid courtiers of Louis XIV and Louis XV.

Pissarro lived at No. 22 on the route de Versailles in Louveciennes. The Marly aqueduct passed behind his house. The route de Versailles was the street that Pissarro most frequently painted in Louveciennes. The earliest painting of it dates from 1869. The picture is, in fact, undated, but it is known that the American dealer and collector, George Lucas, acquired it in January 1870. Pissarro returned to the subject during the following year when Monet also undertook two paintings of the motif, and the road forms the subject of a further picture painted in 1872 after the artist had returned from England. All of these paintings of the route de Versailles dating from the early 1870s explore the device of a road drawn on a steep diagonal, or even at right angles to the picture plane, leading into the composition. Figures move along the road emphasizing its directional flow, but the distribution of trees and houses (including Pissarro's own on the left) at the sides of the road gives breadth to the composition and serves as a horizontal counterpoint. The emphasis on geometry in these pictures is found elsewhere in Pissarro's œuvre at this date and is matched by the short, crisp brushstrokes. Compared with the freedom of Monet's or Sisley's canvases, Pissarro keeps tight control over every aspect of his paintings of the route de Versailles,

Claude Monet (1840-1926). The Versailles Road, Louveciennes, 1870.

and modifies each composition slightly in his eagerness to achieve balance and purity of form. The device of a road leading into a painting is, of course, one used by Dutch landscape painters of the seventeenth century, but both Pissarro and Monet achieve a dramatic tension between the telescoping of the view down the road and the splaying out of the buildings across the canvas. Spatial depth is contrasted with flattened shapes, as in certain Japanese *ukiyo-e* prints that had begun to be imported into France during these years.

Meindert Hobbema (1638-1709). The Avenue, Middelharnis, c. 1689.

Ando Hiroshige (1797-1858). Yoshiwara Gateway with Cherry Trees and Taiya Outside: View Down Street at Night, 1842-1853.

The Versailles Road, Louveciennes, 1872.

Entrance of the Village of Voisins, 1872.

Central to this phase of Pissarro's work is the painting dating from 1870, now in the Bührle Stiftung in Zürich, of this same road in Louveciennes. There are, however, several differences between this painting and others of this period. It is vertical in format and considerably larger. It has a rare personal interest in that it depicts Julie Vellay with the artist's second child, Jeanne, seen in the front garden of their house in conversation with a neighbour. The influence of Monet is overriding as regards colour, brushwork and the concern for the role of the human figure within the composition. It is essentially a figure painting and as such is unique in Pissarro's œuvre at this date. One might conclude that this is Pissarro's response to Monet's *Women in the Garden* and in the history of Impressionism it deserves to have a position of similar importance. There are several occasions in Pissarro's early drawings done in France when he attempts figure compositions: firstly, at La Roche-Guyon in 1859, and secondly at La Varenne-Saint-Hilaire in the 1860s, but these remained untested and were not transferred to canvas. A preparatory drawing in Oxford for the picture in the Bührle Stiftung reveals how Pissarro has reduced the scale of the figure in the foreground and paid close attention to inserting the form into the overall design. The final composition shows the route de Versailles stretching in front of the house with another family seen walking past. This road, together with the fence, serve as one diagonal, counterbalanced by the

implied diagonal connecting the figures in the left foreground, the tree and the house on the other side. While the diagonal extending from lower right to upper left leads the eye into an enclosed space bounded by houses and trees, the other, passing from shadow to sunlight, leads to a landscape of melting beauty over the Ile-de-France. The tree in front of Pissarro's house does not actually mark the centre of the composition, but its spreading branches in the upper half negate the divisions within the picture caused by the interaction of the diagonals. The debt to Monet is perhaps most explicit in the brushwork and colour. The dextrous treatment of the figures on the road and the blooms in the front garden, which, like the blue ribbon in Julie Vellay's hair and the red flower held in her hand, relieve the shadowy foreground, evoke comparison with Monet. Single brushstrokes of pure colour freely applied throughout the picture sustain an evenness of facture that belies the variety within the painting. This is true Impressionism: a radical response, applied with a controlled technique within a measured composition, to the natural beauty of the artist's surroundings.

Compositional Study of an Interior. Pencil.

Study of Julie Vellay with her Daughter in the Front Garden of their House at Louveciennes. Black chalk.

The Versailles Road, Louveciennes, 1870.

This moment of felicitous creativity, however, was interrupted by the Franco-Prussian war. Louveciennes did not escape the Prussian advance and the artist's home was occupied by the invading troops. Pissarro left Louveciennes in a hurry towards the autumn of 1870 and moved by stages to England. He left behind in the house on the route de Versailles all his furniture and twenty years' work estimated at the most at about 1500 items (paintings, *études*, drawings). Apparently, only a very small proportion of this total survived, but it is, as yet, difficult to ascertain how, if at all, these losses should affect our interpretation of the artist's œuvre. Stylistically, however, continuity was maintained and Pissarro, in tandem with Monet, was able to develop his Impressionism further in England. Significantly, in London, as Pissarro later told Dewhurst in his letter of 1902, "Monet worked in the parks, whilst I, living at Lower Norwood, at that time a charming suburb, studied the effects of fog, snow and springtime." It is, in fact, the seasonal, or temporal, aspects of many of the London paintings that impress the viewer: the sharp light and stiff breeze of the painting of the Crystal Palace at Sydenham, the sound of muffled footsteps crunching in the snow covering Lower Norwood, or the morning sun evaporating lingering patches of mist as the sap rises in the trees on an early spring day. Acuity of eye and precision in the touch are the hallmarks of these paintings, which are rendered completely in the Impressionist idiom.

Snow at Lower Norwood, London, 1870.

The Crystal Palace, London, 1871.

Lordship Lane Station, Upper Norwood, London, 1871.

Near Sydenham Hill (with Lower Norwood in the Background), 1871.

J.M.W. Turner (1775-1851).
Rain, Steam and Speed: the Great Western Railway, 1843.

James Bourne (1773-1854).
Construction of the London and Birmingham Railway, 1857. Lithograph.

Train, Bedford Park, London, 1897.

The Road alongside the Railway Line, 1873.

The Railway Crossing at Les Pâtis near Pontoise, 1873-1874.

Two of the paintings done in England have reverberations of a different kind. *Lordship Lane Station*, the first fully elaborated treatment of the train in Impressionist painting, is perhaps a direct comment on J.M.W. Turner's *Rain, Steam and Speed: the Great Western Railway*, then on view in the National Gallery in London. Pissarro remarked, again in the context of Dewhurst's book, "that Turner and Constable, while they taught us something, showed us in their works that they had no understanding of the *analysis of shadow*, which in Turner's painting is simply used as an effect, a mere absence of light. As far as tone division is concerned, Turner proved the value of this as a method, among methods, although he did not apply it correctly and naturally." Pissarro's train draws out of the station towards the cutting with the smoke blowing away from the spectator further into the picture space. This is a dispassionate rendering of Turner's poetic evocation, more in keeping with early prints of railways, such as those by James Bourne. The train in Pissarro's painting forms part of the landscape and is accepted as no more than an integral part of the composition. The artist treated the theme of the train in a landscape on two other occasions much later in his career. These are equally dispassionate, and similarly accept the train as no more than a single element in the composition, whereas in *The Railway Crossing at Les Pâtis*, or *The Railway Line at Pontoise*, the trains are omitted and modern technology is ignored in favour of figures walking through the landscape.

Dulwich College is much looser in handling, especially the pond in the foreground in which the buildings and sky are so prominently reflected. Pissarro seems to have concentrated far more on the textural quality of paint in a way that suggests that he may have subjected the works of John Constable to close scrutiny while in London. Many of the qualities found in *Dulwich College*, however, were retained for paintings at Louveciennes after he had returned to France in the summer of 1871. Pissarro found his house at Louveciennes in chaos. A letter written to him by Julie Vellay's sister, Félicie Estruc, in March 1871 provides an account of the devastation caused by the Prussian occupation: "I went from Rueil to Louveciennes on foot. All the road is in a

Dulwich College, London, 1871.

John Constable (1776-1837). Salisbury Cathedral from the River, 1827.

The Seine at Marly, 1871.

Snow at Louveciennes, 1872.

terrible state. The surface is impassable for vehicles, the houses are burnt, windows, shutters, doors, staircases and floors are all ruined. I arrived at Louveciennes and failed to recognize the house. After looking at them all I went to see M. Ollivon who reassured me a little. He has managed to save a few small things including the two beds, a mattress, your wardrobe, *toilette*, desk, about forty paintings and the little wooden-frame bed. The Prussians lived in the house for nearly four months. They searched for everything, but they failed to find the little cupboard, the one on the upper floor, under the stairs. Everything has been reclaimed by M. Ollivon. He asked me to tell you that you can return now… In Paris it is very quiet. There are no disturbances. Above all, the food supply has returned to what it was before the war. As to your house it is uninhabitable; there is straw throughout, the horses were kept on the ground floor and the Prussian soldiers lived above."

Absence, however, seems to have quickened Pissarro's response to his surroundings in France. *The Seine at Marly-le-Roi* (1871) possesses a freedom of colour and execution that warrants comparison with Monet's and Renoir's paintings of the bathing-places at La Grenouillère. *Snow at Louveciennes* and *Chestnut Trees at Louveciennes* (both 1872) are notable for their luminosity and incandescent shadows; *Landscape with Flooded Fields* and *Landscape, the Harvest, Pontoise*, both painted near Pontoise in 1873, afford a contrast in season: the one with the bare trees of winter calligraphically silhouetted against a cloudy sky and the other with the earth warmed by a summer sun.

The years 1872-1874 were amongst the most successful in Pissarro's career from a strictly artistic point of view. He perfected the style of Impressionism in works of the highest quality and he was winning the confidence of a number of private collectors. Unfortunately, as Duret reminded him in a letter of 1874, these collectors did not have unlimited means and therefore could not make extensive purchases from the Impressionists. Although financially the first half of the 1870s did not prove too exacting, the second half was one of great personal deprivation. Pissarro, Sisley and Monet suffered financial hardship, which intensified with the public vilification caused by the group exhibitions.

52

Chestnut Trees at Louveciennes, 1872.

Pissarro had returned from England in late June 1871, but only lived in Louveciennes for just over one more year. In August 1872 he moved back to Pontoise. Although this did not induce an immediate change in style, it heralded an important shift that will be examined in the next chapter. Ironically, this shift is apparent in the selection of five paintings Pissarro made for the first Impressionist exhibition. Four of these (*Orchard in Bloom, Hoar-Frost, Chestnut Trees at Osny*, and *June Morning, Pontoise*) are undeniably Impressionist in style, but *Public Park, Pontoise* is a transitional work.

Landscape, the Harvest, Pontoise, 1873.

Hoar Frost, the Old Road to Ennery, Pontoise, 1873.

The Sente de Justice, Pontoise, c. 1872.

Israel Silvestre (1621-1691).
View of Pontoise. Engraving.

Camille Pissarro and the Crisis of Impressionism

CAMILLE PISSARRO'S life and work are closely associated with Pontoise. He lived there between 1866-1868 and again from 1872-1882. The town lies to the north-west of Paris marking the border of two regions of northern France—the Vexin, of which it was the capital, and the Ile-de-France. As can be seen in Pissarro's general views of the town, Pontoise is situated on the top of an escarpment overlooking the valley of Montmorency with a commanding view of the plain below leading towards Paris. During the medieval period Pontoise was of immense strategic and historical importance, particularly for the Capetian and Valois kings in their struggle against the Angevins and Plantagenets of England. It was the place from whence Louis IX launched his crusade, but the real significance of Pontoise stemmed from its geographical position, which granted it a dual character. Its hilltop position meant that it was a good fortress and the river Oise, on the banks of which it was also situ-

ated, made it an inland port for barges. Pontoise, therefore, was blessed with some distinguished medieval architecture and thrived as a commercial town. By the beginning of the nineteenth century, however, mainly as a result of the Revolution of 1789, Pontoise had declined. In fact, its population had decreased to a level below that of the thirteenth century. Yet, throughout the nineteenth century there was a gradual process of modernization, redevelopment and industrialization. A design for the urban development of Pontoise by Théodore Muller dating from 1864 indicates how the town was changing. The purpose was to join the newly built railway station to the centre, symbolized by the church of Saint-Maclou. In order to do this a new road was built (formerly the rue l'Imperiale, now the rue Thiers) connecting the station in the foreground of the lithograph to Saint-Maclou. What the lithograph and ordinary maps of Pontoise do not show, however, is the hilly terrain on which the town stands. The rue

Pontoise, Quai du Pothuis, 1868.

View of Pontoise, Banks of the Oise, 1872.

The Crossroads, Pontoise, 1872.

View of Pontoise, 1873.

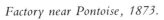

Factory near Pontoise, 1873.

The Gisors Road, Pontoise, Snow, 1873.

Thiers is, in fact, fairly steep and different parts of the town are on separate levels. This is an aspect of Pontoise that Pissarro particularly relished and, indeed, exploited in his work. The lithograph, however, does show other important areas of Pontoise: the church of Notre-Dame half seen at the left edge, the public garden in the upper left corner near the Parc-aux-Charettes, the river Oise with the Ile de Pothuis and the factory of Chalon et Cie on the other bank at the right edge in the upper half, and, finally, in that same area, but on the town side, the semi-rural part known as L'Hermitage where Pissarro lived for many of the years he spent in Pontoise. Economically, the railway eclipsed the canal system, while granaries, tanneries and distilleries supplanted the numerous local mills. Yet, although the threat of industrialization hung over Pontoise, its basic economy did not change—subsistence farming and market-gardening. With the growth of Paris in the nineteenth century, places like Pontoise within easy reach of the metropolis became important as suppliers. Agriculture, therefore, was an expanding industry in the regions around Pontoise. The grain fields stretched northwards towards Ennery, while the fruit and vegetable (root crops) farms were often adjacent to houses owned or rented by those who worked these small patches so intensely. These are the *jardins potagers* that are so often depicted by Pissarro.

Pontoise, therefore, provided a variety of themes for Pissarro. It was a mixed economy with factories being established on the banks of the Oise towards Saint-Ouen-l'Aumône and a host of market-gardens. His earliest representations of the town reveal its duality, for, while he was painting the group of landscapes of L'Hermitage submitted to the Salon, he also painted two views of the Quai du Pothuis in the centre of the town. The earlier one now in Tel-Aviv, dating from 1867, shows in the background the chimney stack of a small factory on the boulevard des Fossés extending above the hillsides behind. Pissarro painted a similar composition one year later, shifting his viewpoint slightly in order to incorporate the chimney of the newly opened gasworks. This chimney is given prominence by the fact that it is centrally placed on a line with the bourgeois figures walking along the *quai*. This pic-

Théodore Muller (1819-1879).
Design for an urban project in Pontoise, 1864. Lithograph.

ture is the closest Pissarro comes to the cityscapes of Paris painted by Renoir and Monet during these same years. A more general view of the town, probably painted in 1872, not only emphasizes the hilly terrain, but also offsets the chimney of the gasworks and the lantern of the church of Notre-Dame against the pathway, the trees and the fence. This painting is axiomatic of his attitude to Pontoise, neatly combining the rural with the industrial. He balances out the vertical forms of the chimney, the lantern of the church and the tree almost as symbols of contrasting ways of life that were representative of Pontoise, if not of France as a whole. The interplay between rural life and urban life, found in microcosm in Pontoise, became a dominant theme in Pissarro's work during the 1890s and was not limited to one particular place, but ranged throughout his œuvre.

Apart from when he explores special motifs over a number of years, such as the factory of Chalon et Cie, Pissarro's depiction of Pontoise is notable for its absence of traditionally admired picturesque motifs. The churches usually form no more than the background to paintings; the larger houses, with one notable exception, and the *châteaux* in the surrounding districts are virtually ignored; the medieval architecture found in the town rarely occurs. Pissarro, in short, does not set out to portray Pontoise in a topographical sense, but decided instead to characterize it by emphasizing its more general appearance and its more ordinary occurrences viewed, as at Louveciennes, in its streets. The *Crossroads at Pontoise*, for example, is a composition that balances the large expanse of sky with the empty foreground. The eye is delayed by the road in the front of the picture before gathering speed down the incline, at which point it suddenly meets the row of houses that dominates the middle distance. Pissarro, it has been said, is a painter of the middle distance. It is there that the various parts of a composition fuse together and where the painter's organizational power is seen to best advantage. The tension that Pissarro found in the differing levels of Pontoise is the key to his stylistic development during the second half of the 1870s and it proved to be of particular importance in his friendship with Cézanne.

Peasant Woman pushing a Wheelbarrow, the Rondest House, Pontoise, 1874.

Portrait of Cézanne, 1874.

"In order to make progress, there is only nature, and the eye is trained in contact with her," Cézanne wrote in 1904. But this was not an emotional response to nature, as with the Romantics. It was a strictly cerebral examination. "I progress very slowly, for nature reveals herself to me in very complex ways; and the progress needed is endless" (1904). Just looking at nature, therefore, was not enough. It was the way the artist looked at nature and what he chose to see in nature that was also of vital importance. Both men regarded the *sensations* experienced before nature as being of cardinal significance, but the struggle began with the need to reduce those *sensations* to articulate forms. What nature suggested, then, was a series of shapes, mathematical or otherwise. For both artists this perpetual reference to nature amounted to a lifetime's absorption.

"One strives in vain," wrote Pissarro to Lucien in February 1894. "What is necessary is to prepare the ground with truly *felt* works, and one's reputation takes care of itself. There is no better method, everything else is superfluous. Long hair, dandyism, noise, count for nothing; work, observation and sensation are the only real forces." Cézanne wrote separately to two young painters, Emile Bernard in 1904 and Louis Aurenche in 1905: "I remain in the grip of sense-perceptions and, in spite of my age, riveted to painting"; and "I work all the time and that without paying any attention to criticism and the critics, as a real artist should proceed. My work must prove that I am right."

These shared attitudes found expression not just in their work, but also in their representations of each other. Pissarro's *Portrait of Cézanne* (1874), for example, shows Cézanne seated in country clothes in a room on the wall of which are two political cartoons arranged in the upper corners of the picture above a landscape by Pissarro. The political caricatures represent polarities within French politics during those years—Thiers, the conservative, confronted by Courbet, the radical—but it should be observed that Cézanne sits with his back to them. More significant is his manner of dress, implying that the domain of art lay beyond the realm prescribed by urban life. This is the artist as *ouvrier*, turning his back on society and waging his own individual struggle with life—a slightly sinister variant of the landscape

Pissarro had met Paul Cézanne at the Académie Suisse during the early 1860s. Cézanne, too, had been born many miles away from Paris. He, too, had experienced parental opposition to his desire to become a painter. He had also received some academic training in Aix-en-Provence and had a deep sense of respect for the art of the past, making numerous "free" copies of a whole range of artists. "The Louvre is a good book to consult, but it must be only an intermediary. The real and immense study to be undertaken is the manifold picture of nature," he wrote in May 1904 to Emile Bernard. Such statements would have been in full accord with Pissarro's own opinions and the two artists held many other ideas in common. Cézanne's letters contain numerous statements that echo, complement, or develop ideas found in Pissarro's letters. Chief amongst these reflections is the supremacy of nature.

A Square at La Roche-Guyon, c. 1867.

Still Life, 1867.

artist described by Frédéric Henriet in *Le paysagiste aux champs* (1866). Contemporary photographs of both Pissarro and Cézanne, from one of which Cézanne made a drawing of his fellow artist, depict the stout boots, hat and packed equipment that both men wore during the mid-1870s. They almost resemble mountaineers and thereby unconsciously foreshadow the ideas expressed by the French anarchist philosopher Elisée Reclus, whose book entitled *The History of a Mountain* (1880) Pissarro most probably read.

The close working friendship between Pissarro and Cézanne lasted over two decades (from 1861 until the early 1880s) and was to prove of the utmost significance for the development of European art. "To my mind," Cézanne wrote to Roger Marx in 1905, "one does not put oneself in place of the past, one only adds a new link." Early pictures by Pissarro painted with the palette knife, *The Square at La Roche-Guyon* and a *Still Life*, both dating from the late 1860s, are directly comparable with paintings of the same decade by Cézanne. It is not simply a matter of the technical similarities, but also of the spatial sense applying to both compositions. The internal rhythms set up by the buildings in the *Square at La Roche-Guyon* and the seemingly haphazard disposition of the objects in the *Still Life* create a visual tension and a quickened response in the viewer that surpass mere representational art. Yet, such comparisons or, alternatively, the juxtaposition of those direct copies made by Cézanne after Pissarro's paintings, do not really reveal all that much about the intentions of the two men. More important, perhaps, is the realization that Cézanne's approach to landscape was governed by Pissarro's paintings of the late 1860s and that a great deal of their work together during the 1870s amounted to a re-examination of those areas of Pontoise which had first attracted Pissarro. They occasionally painted the same motifs and together they explored other motifs along the valley of the Oise towards Valmondois, Valhermeil and Auvers-sur-Oise, the home of a mutual friend, Dr. Paul Gachet. As will be seen, this terrain resembled that of L'Hermitage and Les Pâtis very closely. The inclination of both men was the slow and gradual assimilation of a clearly defined area of landscape. The way Pissarro had looked at L'Hermitage was, in fact, the way that Cézanne later came to look at the countryside surrounding Aix-en-Provence. As Cézanne wrote to his own son from Aix towards the very end of his life, "Finally I must tell you that as a painter I am becoming more clear sighted before nature, but that with me the realization of my sensations is always painful. I cannot attain the intensity that is unfolded before my senses… Here on the bank of the river the motifs multiply, the same subject seen from a different angle offers subject for study of the most powerful interest and so varied that I think I could occupy myself for months without changing place, by turning now more to the right, now more to the left."

Thus, as regards the mid-1870s, Cézanne painted a composition, apparently of the Côte du Jallais, that recalls *Landscape at Les Pâtis*, while Pissarro himself

Paul Cézanne (1839-1906). Houses at Valhermeil, 1879-1882.

repeated the composition of *Côte du Jallais* in a looser and broader style. A comparison, however, between *L'Hermitage, Pontoise* and *Houses at Valhermeil* by Cézanne, reveals exactly what the latter considered to be so important about Pissarro's paintings of the late 1860s. The houses, compactly arranged at the foot of the hillside, have a precisely calculated structural significance within the composition. Their end walls, their roofs and gables are set at different angles contrasting sharply with the less regulated lines of the surrounding countryside. Once more, it is these houses placed in the middle distance that determine the character and layout of the whole composition. *Houses at Valhermeil* shares with Pissarro's canvases of the late 1860s a concern for vertical and horizontal axes, a predilection for carefully structured compositions organized in parallel layers and a predominance of sharply defined solid forms. These are features that Cézanne clearly owed to the example of Pissarro, although he may have refined them by looking at Poussin. The difference between the two painters lay in the rigour with which Cézanne applied the method, paring down a particular landscape to its essential parts with such ruthless ability that Pissarro remarked to the young Matisse that "Cézanne is not an impressionist painter because all his life he has been painting the same picture."

Another motif involving the handling of spatial intervals within a composition that Cézanne might have explored with Pissarro can be found at La Roche-Guyon. Topographical accounts of the Seine frequently

La Côte du Jallais (Jallais Hill), Pontoise, 1875.

The examination of spatial intervals within a composition was not the only aspect of their art that Pissarro and Cézanne developed while working together during the mid–1870s. There was also the question of stylistic and technical innovations developed in order to depict the landscape more convincingly. The relationship between the various parts in *La Sente de Justice, Pontoise* by Pissarro is successful in a purely descriptive sense, but the same technique would not be wholly possible for a more severe pictorial analysis. Cézanne's own treatment of a similar motif, this time at Auvers-sur-Oise, illustrates the limitations of Pissarro's approach. Cézanne told Bernard in 1904 that "nature for us is more depth than surface." What interested Pissarro and Cézanne technically, therefore, was the means of obtaining a unified composition by a more deliberate juxtaposition of brushstrokes on the canvas. Spatial depth was to be based on facture and colour. This resulted in a tendency towards regularized brushstrokes sometimes broadly applied with a flat brush in blocks. The palette is often limited and the interrelationship between various parts of the picture created by tonal nuances.

La Roche-Guyon, c. 1866. Etching.

refer to the medieval castle overlooking La Roche-Guyon built at the summit of a geological outcrop. Pissarro had first essayed this subject in an early etching of the mid–1860s and another etching of La Roche-Guyon (c. 1880) shows that the place continued to interest him, as it did Renoir and Monet. Cézanne's paintings of *The Turn in the Road* are of La Roche-Guyon and may be regarded as a development of Pissarro's earlier etching. This progression from the undemonstrative composition by Pissarro to the much more articulate and firmer representation of space in Cézanne's composition was in turn evolved further by Georges Braque in an early cubist painting of La Roche-Guyon executed not long after he had returned from a painting campaign in L'Estaque where his work had undergone the clear influence of Cézanne.

La Roche-Guyon. Pencil.

The Quarry, Pontoise, c. 1875.

La Roche-Guyon. Wood engraving from Charles Nodier,
La Seine et ses bords, 1836.

Paul Cézanne (1839-1906).
Still Life with Skull and Candlestick, 1865-1867.

Paul Cézanne (1839-1906).
The Hanged Man's House, Auvers-sur-Oise, 1872-1873.

Paul Cézanne (1839-1906).La Côte du Galet (Galet Hill), Pontoise, 1879-1882.

Nicolas Poussin (1594-1665).Christ healing the Blind Man, 1650.

Photograph of Cézanne (left) and Pissarro (right) ▷
at Pontoise in the 1870s.

Paul Cézanne (1839-1906). Pissarro with ▷▷
Walking Stick and Knapsack, c. 1877. Pencil.

Paul Cézanne (1839-1906). View of Auvers-sur-Oise, 1879-1882.

Paul Cézanne (1839-1906). Houses in Provence, 1880-1885.

Paul Cézanne (1839-1906).
L'Etang des Sœurs, Pontoise, 1875-1877.

Georges Braque (1882-1963).
La Roche-Guyon, 1909.

The Little Bridge, Pontoise, 1875.

Several of Pissarro's canvases attest the experiments made by Cézanne right into the 1880s. The tendency to flatten the composition may be witnessed in *Bourgeois House at L'Hermitage* or *Public Park, Pontoise* (both 1873), but the more regularized brushstroke, aided perhaps by a return to the use of the palette knife, only begins to appear in 1875 with *The Saint-Antoine Road at L'Hermitage, The Quarry* or *The Village Pathway*. It is probable that by this time both Pissarro and Cézanne were again examining works by Courbet. This is particularly the case in *The Little Bridge, Pontoise* (1875), which is essentially a *sous-bois* motif not dissimilar to Cézanne's own *L'Etang des Sœurs, Pontoise*. In both, the light filtered through the foliage and the reflections on the water are depicted with horizontal strokes from which emerges a sense of depth within the composition. *The Little Bridge* anticipates Cézanne's *Bridge at Maincy* (c. 1879), which Pissarro knew, since he made a brief pencil drawing of it, and all these paintings, significantly, bring to mind a phrase used by Cézanne in a letter from Aix-en-Provence to his son in 1906: "There are some large trees, they form a vault over the water."

The extent to which Pissarro developed this method of painting is perhaps best represented in *The Climbing Path, L'Hermitage*, which may instructively be compared with *La Sente de Justice, Pontoise*. The high viewpoint over the pathway across to the houses on the other side of the dip, the glance down over the roof of the house below, the precipitous path extending up the right edge of the composition, and the overlapping of the different types of foliage partake of a spatial disequilibrium that yet carries conviction as a result of the application of paint. Many of Cézanne's canvases dating from the mid-1870s have a variety of brushstroke, but sometimes contained within them are signs that he was moving towards the more regularized stroke, so often referred to as the "constructive stroke." *View of Auvers-sur-Oise* exhibits a host of different strokes made with brushes of various sizes, yet the control exercised over parts of the middle distance reveals that a painting such as *View of Valhermeil* or *Zola's Villa at Médan* would soon be achieved. There are indications that Pissarro also experimented with even strokes. Careful examination of two unfinished works, *Portrait of Madame Pissarro* and *Landscape at Osny*, both of uncertain date, shows extensive passages of regulated strokes—over the skirt in the portrait, but existing throughout the landscape. Osny is a small village near Pontoise where Pissarro lived in 1882–1883. The facture and the treatment of the landscape are possibly an

Paul Cézanne (1839-1906). The Bridge at Maincy, c. 1879.

The Climbing Path, L'Hermitage, Pontoise, 1875.

Portrait of Madame Pissarro, sketch, c. 1874.

exercise by Pissarro using Cézanne's "constructive stroke" and again the composition refers back to the all–important *L'Hermitage at Pontoise* of 1867.

It is no exaggeration to say that Pissarro and Cézanne together laid the foundations of modern painting during the second half of the 1870s. It was as much an intellectual effort as a technical one and it was as much a pooling of resources as an individual achievement. Any influence between the two artists was reciprocal. Cézanne towards the end of his life could describe Pissarro in a letter as "humble and colossal," while Pissarro championed Cézanne's work ceaselessly. As early as 1872 he wrote to Guillemet, "Our Cézanne raised our hopes and I have seen his paintings; I have with me here a painter of great force, of remarkable strength. If, as I hope, he settles for some time in Auvers where he is going to live, he will certainly surprise those artists who have too hastily condemned him." Even as late as 1933 Gertrude Stein, referring to Paris in 1903–1907, could write in *The Autobiography of Alice B. Toklas* that "Pissarro indeed was the man from whom all the early Cézanne lovers heard about Cézanne." In his turn Cézanne remarked, as J.M.W. Turner had done of Thomas Girtin, that "If Pissarro

had continued to paint the way he did in 1870, he would have surpassed all of us."

During the early 1860s Pissarro had met at the Académie Suisse another painter whose life became inextricably bound up with his own. Ludovic Piette had been a pupil of Thomas Couture and a friend with Pissarro of the landscape painter Antoine Chintreuil, who worked with Corot. A large representation of Piette's work was included in the third Impressionist exhibition (1877) and was also shown posthumously in the fourth Impressionist exhibition (1879). His friendship with Pissarro was to prove of crucial importance after 1874, owing to the financial relief that Piette offered by extending hospitality to the painter and his family at Montfoucault near Melleray in Mayenne where Piette's family farmed. Pissarro went to Montfoucault in the autumn of each year from 1874-1877, a series of visits that was only brought to a close by Piette's death in 1878. These were years of perpetual financial hardship and several passages of near despair occur in the artist's letters, perhaps not only caused by penury, but also by some uncertainty as to how best to develop the tenets of Impressionist painting. Pissarro wrote to his friend Eugène Murer: "It is no longer bearable. Everything I do ends in failure... When will I get out of this mess and

Landscape at Osny, sketch, c. 1884.

The Kitchen at Piette's Farm, Montfoucault, 1874.

be able to give myself with tranquillity to my work? My studies are made without method, without joy, without spirit because of my feeling that I must abandon art and try to do something else—if it is possible to serve a new apprenticeship. Sad!" This feeling of dejection and the lack of a sense of direction was experienced by most of the artists involved with the Impressionist movement. Some were driven in these adverse financial circumstances to submit their works to the official Salon in order to obtain recognition and facilitate the sale of their paintings. Renoir, Monet, Cézanne and Sisley resorted to this, and Pissarro may have done so, given the large size of *The Backwoods at L'Hermitage, Pontoise* (1879). The cohesion felt at the time of the first Impressionist exhibition was slowly evaporating and was challenged equally by the painters themselves, as well as by such critics as Zola. Pissarro, however, continued to be a calming influence tirelessly negotiating between the various factions as the exhibitions of 1876, 1877 and 1879 were being planned.

Pissarro's anxieties during these years may have been increased by his attempt to come to terms with fresh subject matter. As has been seen, his friendship with Cézanne led to experiments in compositional and technical matters, which he was able to apply for the rest of the decade, but the critic Théodore Duret advised Pissarro on the subject matter of his pictures. Duret wrote to Pissarro in December 1873: "I persist in thinking that rustic nature with animals is what suits your talent best. You haven't Sisley's decorative feeling, nor Monet's fantastic eye, but you have what they have not, an intimate and profound feeling for nature and a power of brush, with the result that a beautiful picture by you is something absolutely definitive. If I had a piece of advice to give you, I should say: don't think of Monet or of Sisley, don't pay attention to what they are doing, go your own way, your path of rural nature. You will be going along a new road, as far and as high as any master. I find now that I have four paintings of yours, which more or less have the same horizon line and rural motifs that are a little sad. It is surely necessary to replace that with a little variety and to introduce a new note." Pissarro replied almost immediately. "Thank your for your advice. You should know that I have thought about what you said for a long time. What has prevented me for so long from painting nature in the raw is simply that I have not had any models at my disposal, not just to make a painting, but also for studying the subject seriously. For the rest, I will not delay attempting it any further. It will be very difficult. As you must realize, these paintings cannot always be done from nature, that is to say in the open. It will certainly be difficult."

Thomas Gainsborough (1727-1788). The Watering Place, 1775.

The Farm at Montfoucault, 1874.

The Pond at Montfoucault, 1875.

Peasant Woman Carding Wool, 1875.

Yet, the autumn seasons in Montfoucault, so different from the rural environment of Pontoise, provided Pissarro with exactly the motifs and facilities he needed. The paintings he executed in Mayenne are therefore not only a reconsideration of the achievement of Jean-François Millet, Pissarro's famous predecessor in peasant subjects, but they are also painted in a style that continues to test the ideas discussed with Cézanne. In December 1874 Pissarro faithfully reported to Duret: "I haven't worked badly here, applying myself to figures and animals. I have attempted several genre scenes, but I approach this branch of art timidly, since so much of this kind of work has been done by artists of the first rank. I am terrified that I will make a complete mess of it."

Pissarro did, indeed, discover new motifs at Montfoucault and essayed a whole realm of fresh subjects related to rural life. At first, in two paintings of the farmyard at Montfoucault, for instance, the compositions are carefully constructed. The buildings are judiciously framed by the trees and the figures are precisely related to the background. *The Farm at Montfoucault* now in Geneva was, in fact, exhibited in the second Impressionist exhibition. Matching these paintings of 1874 in their somewhat cautious approach are the genre scenes showing the interior of the farm at Montfoucault. Other paintings, by contrast, are more broadly painted so that both *The Pond at Montfoucault* and *The Harvest* are heavily worked. *The Pond at Montfoucault* is a picture redolent of the European landscape tradition, evoking comparisons with Thomas Gainsborough's *Watering Place*, which Pissarro could have seen in London in 1870-1871, as well as with more recent artists of the Barbizon school—Constant Troyon. Pissarro creates a feeling of recession by overlaying different parts of the composition. The cows and the figure are silhouetted against the pond and the foliage against the opposite bank and the sky. The tree in full autumnal splendour on the left—its golden leaves recalling the golden shower falling on Danae—marks the middle distance dividing foreground and background with its spreading branches. *The Harvest* also makes use of prominently placed objects, such as corn stacks and the tall tree, to create a sense of distance. Generally, however, Pissarro concentrates his attention on rural labour. There are far fewer pure landscapes dating from the Montfoucault years, but this study of the human figure was only to reach fruition during the next decade. Individual figures, other than members of his own family, now often form the subject of paintings, in a series of portraits of local people, perhaps shyly agreeing to pose for the artist. Alternatively, Pissarro could observe the completion of the harvest in the farmyard with groups of figures busily engaged in tossing the hay and building a hay stack.

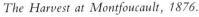

The Harvest at Montfoucault, 1876.

La Côte des Bœufs, Pontoise, 1877.

Kitchen Garden and Trees in Flower, Spring, Pontoise, 1877.

The seasons spent painting at Montfoucault had two results. Firstly, he had an opportunity to study rural life at first hand. This was to be significant in the long term when Pissarro moved from Pontoise further into the country to Eragny-sur-Epte and began for the second time to paint rural subjects. Secondly, the range of colour within the pictures undertaken at Montfoucault increases considerably and, together with the technical advances made in the company of Cézanne, allowed Pissarro to achieve those outstanding landscapes that bring the 1870s to a glorious close. Amongst these are *Côte des Bœufs, Pontoise*, which is in turn related to

The Red Roofs, L'Hermitage and *Sous-bois Landscape, L'Hermitage*, and *Kitchen Garden in Flower, Spring*. In each of these paintings the myriad colours and the intricacy of the composition fully demonstrate Pissarro's skills as a colourist. The eye is absorbed within each composition and is engaged in separating the numerous layers of paint. When *The Pathway at Le Chou*, amongst several other works, was exhibited at the sixth Impressionist exhibition (1881), the novelist and critic Joris-Karl Huysmans wrote enthusiastically of Pissarro's skills as a landscape painter: "*The Pathway at Le Chou* is a landscape where a patchy sky extends to infinity, bro-

The Pathway at Le Chou, Pontoise, 1878.

The Backwoods at L'Hermitage, Pontoise, 1879.

ken only by the tree-tops, and where a river runs, near which factory chimneys smoke and pathways cross woodlands. It is the landscape of a powerful colourist who has at last grasped and overcome the terrible difficulties of painting in full daylight in the open. It is the new formula which has been sought for a long time and has now been fully realized; the true countryside at last emerges from this assembly of classically mixed colours and there is in this natural scene so bathed in air, a great calm, a serene fulfilment descending with the sun; an enveloping peace issuing from this quite ordinary site whose brilliant tones spread themselves out over a vast firmament upwards to the peaceful clouds... M. Pissarro may now be classed among the number of remarkable and audacious painters we possess. If he can preserve his perceptive, delicate, and nimble eye, we shall certainly have in him the most original landscapist of our time."

Yet, Pissarro himself despaired of this particular style that he had gradually developed during the second half of the 1870s. He likened it to "knitting" and sought to change it. The boldest demonstration of this closely wrought style is perhaps *The Backwoods at L'Hermitage*, a large painting which he may have hoped to submit to the Salon. Here the web of brushstrokes and the varying tones of green lead the eye through the glade to the houses beyond. The goat and the man lying on the ground in the centre are almost lost in the undergrowth below the tall thin trees amidst the patches of dappled light. During these years of the crisis of Impressionism it is salutary to look back and to compare *The Backwoods at L'Hermitage* with Renoir's *Portrait of Jules Le Cœur in the Forest of Fontainebleau* (1866) or with Sisley's *Alley of Chestnut Trees near La Celle-Saint-Cloud* (1867), where the eye is arrested by the immediate surface of the painting and not drawn further and further into the composition by each successive stroke. It is difficult to understand now why Pissarro should have been dissatisfied with this style, but for him it must have seemed like an unsought-for summation and his instinct was to escape from what appeared to be a cul-de-sac.

Auguste Renoir (1841-1919).
Portrait of Jules Le Cœur in the Forest of Fontainebleau, 1866.

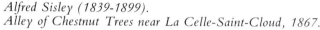

Alfred Sisley (1839-1899).
Alley of Chestnut Trees near La Celle-Saint-Cloud, 1867.

Seated Peasant Woman, 1885.

The Woman on the Road, 1879.
Aquatint with etching and drypoint.

New Interests:
New Horizons

HE CHARGE that is sometimes made dismissing Camille Pissarro as a monotonous or limited artist is totally refuted by the range exhibited in his work of the decade 1880-1890. The difficulties he was experiencing towards the end of the previous decade were shared by nearly all of the Impressionist painters. Each reacted independently to this situation, but, nonetheless, shared the same artistic problems, namely the relationship between the figure and its setting, the question of technique and the whole system of working procedures. As we have seen, in his correspondence with Théodore Duret, Pissarro stressed the difficulty of working *en plein air*. Ironically, just as Edmond Duranty in his important pamphlet *La nouvelle peinture* (1876) described the purpose of Impressionist painting as "to take away the partition separating the studio from everyday life… to make the painter leave his sky-lighted cell… and to bring him out among men in the world," those same artists were, in

fact, contemplating returning into their studio, in order to work from posed models and to devise complicated compositions that involved long and protracted periods of gestation. It is perhaps significant that Degas, who had never really left his studio and who prided himself upon the complexity of his art, should have exerted a considerable influence on the course of French painting at this very moment.

Pissarro's art, therefore, changes direction at the beginning of the 1880s, but it is important to realize that the basic principles underlying it remained the same. The necessity of experiencing sensations before nature and the careful structuring of the compositions continue as recognizable features in Pissarro's output, but the way in which these methods are applied and the context in which they are employed differ. It is these novel aspects of Pissarro's work that make him such an interesting and such an influential artist after 1880. His alliance with painters of the emerging generation

—Gauguin, Van Gogh, Seurat, Signac—gave him a pivotal role in French art of the last quarter of the nineteenth century. It is, in brief, at this stage of his life that Pissarro's sphere of influence matches his personal appearance, as he becomes a truly patriarchal figure.

The shift in Pissarro's art that occurred at the close of the 1870s is reflected in his interest in new techniques and formats, a fresh approach to his subject matter and a willingness to learn from the latest theories in painting advanced by younger artists. Where other Impressionist artists at the beginning of the 1880s sought inspiration by travelling further afield—Monet to the Midi and Renoir to North Africa and Italy—Pissarro subjected his style to close examination and sought a solution through self-analysis. George Moore in his *Reminiscences of the Impressionist Painters* (1906) could not have been more mistaken than when he wrote that "Pissarro always followed in somebody's footsteps, he was a sort of will-o'-the-wisp of painting, and his course was zig-zag." In fact, few painters have been so resolute and determined in the pursuit of their aims. His importance was precisely that he remained a constant in a period of great change and that he was able to come to terms with originality, being quick to detect hypocrisy of any kind. Wide experience, indisputable artistic integrity and a warm personality were the qualities that attracted younger artists to Pissarro at a time when his own art was undergoing change.

It was often the case that when Pissarro was experiencing stylistic difficulties in his paintings he sought for the solution in other media. The artist's own disappointments with his paintings of the late 1870s resulted, perhaps rather surprisingly, in advances being made in his printmaking. Like Degas, Pissarro was a prolific printmaker. Although he had become a member of the *Société des Aquafortistes* in 1863, he never exhibited any of his work under its auspices. Yet, his association with the *Société*, however tentative, is recognizable in the small group of early prints dating from before 1879. These etchings and lithographs are notable for their traditional techniques. The etchings in particular are comparable with those made by the Barbizon painters, specifically Corot and Daubigny. Pissarro cherishes cleanly bitten lines and aims for direct, lyrical images.

The *Société des Aquafortistes* had, in fact, been founded only in 1862. Its purpose was to revive the importance of etching, deriving its main inspiration from Rembrandt, whose influence can be seen in several of Pissarro's own etchings, notably *The Negress* (1867), *Grandmother* (1889-1891) and *Self-Portrait* (1890-1891). Significantly, two of the leading members of the *Société des Aquafortistes* were Alfred Cadart and Auguste Delâtre, print dealer and printer *(imprimeur-artiste)* respectively. Their involvement symbolized a wider debate in printmaking circles as to just where the creative emphasis in the etching process should be placed—on the artist who conceives the design, or the professional printer who inks the plate and pulls the impression. Opinions varied as to whether a print was the result of a collaborative effort between artist and printer, or whether such a system only succeeded in

The Negress, 1867. Etching.

negating the intentions of both. Although Pissarro had to rely on professional printers, such as Auguste Delâtre, Charles Jacque and Salmon until 1894 when he obtained his own press, he was reluctant to do so. Beyond any practical considerations arising from such a division of labour, there were also aesthetic implications involving a separation of "natural" etching, in which tone depended upon the manipulation of line, from "artificial" etching, which relied for tone upon the freer distribution of ink. The "artificial" method was nurtured by *retroussage*, whereby the plate was wiped with a rag spreading the ink across its surface. This method, too, was developed in emulation of Rembrandt, but by the nineteenth century it amounted to improvisation. From this situation there developed the concept of the *peintre-graveur*, the printmaker who experimented with the tonal qualities that could be obtained on a metal plate with a rag or finger and by the application of a variety of grounds. The *peintre-graveur* was no longer simply a painter who engraved, but a magician who worked with acid and ink on a metal plate, creating special effects by unorthodox methods, and who, if possible, pulled the prints for himself. The collaboration between Degas and Pissarro, partly directed towards the intended publication of a journal entitled *Le Jour et la Nuit* illustrated with original prints, resulted in some of the most visually exciting prints of the period. Such accepted methods as soft-ground etching and aquatint were combined with grounds comprising salt, sugar and resin, sometimes applied in conjunction with more traditionally etched or drypoint lines. *Wooded Landscape at L'Hermitage* (1879), for example, can be followed through some six states in which Pissarro has worked on the plate incessantly. The composition relates directly to a contemporary painting and is therefore a good example of how Pissarro was seeking in the printmaking process a clearer exposition of the motifs explored in the *sous-bois* pictures of 1877 *(Côte des Bœufs* and *The Red Roofs)* and 1879 *(The Backwoods at L'Hermitage)*. Similar granular techniques were used for *Horizontal Landscape* (1879), but *The Woman on the Road* (1879) is far looser in its application of the aquatint, which has caused the ink to settle like pools on the surface.

Self-Portrait, 1890-1891. Etching.

Many of the prints dating from these years of collaboration with Degas towards the end of the 1870s and the beginning of the 1880s are known in several states, so that the artist's changes to the plate can be closely followed. This was a matter of some consequence for Impressionist art, since a series of changing images promoted a proper understanding of the idea of a particular scene or object observed over a period of time. Monet during the 1890s attempted a similar task when he began to paint in series, but, in effect, Degas and Pissarro by stressing the importance of all the intermediary states of a print, as opposed to the resulting superiority of the final state, were also recording separate, but related, visual experiences. *Twilight with Haystacks* is a supreme example of the examination of the fluctuations of light and atmosphere in a landscape. The few etched lines that anchor the composition are almost completely enveloped by the aquatint, creating a fluidity of movement within the scene that suggests the passing of time. The real mastery, however, lies in the decision to print this plate in different coloured inks, so that each impression appears to be very different, implying a sequence of events, as opposed to one arrested moment. The importance accorded each individual state is apparent from the fact that several artists included sections of prints in the fifth Impressionist exhibition (1880). The most "painterly" of all the techniques used by Pissarro was another also most probably introduced to him by Degas, who had exhibited several monotypes in the third Impressionist exhibition (1877). The monotype technique involved painting the design onto the plate literally with the brush dipped in a heavy greasy ink, or else "wiping" the design onto a prepared surface, working from dark to light. Considerable skill was needed to pull a print from the plate and the number of impressions was often limited, but the medium had the advantage of spontaneity and strong chiaroscural effects could be gained. The years 1879-1880, therefore, mark a particularly active period of printmaking in Pissarro's career. Working alongside Degas encouraged Pissarro to be inventive and experimental.

Twilight with Haystacks, 1879.
Aquatint with etching and drypoint.

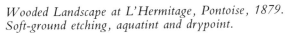

Wooded Landscape at L'Hermitage, Pontoise, 1879.
Soft-ground etching, aquatint and drypoint.

Although Pissarro's prints dating from after this short period of intense activity show no drop in quality, they are more limited in technical range, the favoured medium being *manière grise*, or grey ground, which formed part of the etching process and helped to give the etched lines a richer quality. There are a number of etchings in colour, but it is only in the lithographs of female bathers dating from the 1890s that the earlier freedom and confidence experienced while working with Degas again becomes apparent.

Allied to this fascination for new printing techniques was Pissarro's concern for pastel, gouache and tempera. Sometimes prints are heightened with these media, but more often he adopted these crumbly techniques for drawings, paintings and fans, which he hoped would result in quicker sales. Pissarro first exhibited fans at the fourth Impressionist exhibition (1879) where he included twelve out of a total of thirty-seven works. Fans, ostensibly produced as a cheaper art form, were made by Pissarro throughout the 1880s, but there is a reduction in number after 1890. The fan was mainly associated with the eighteenth century, but in revitalizing an interest in the format Degas and Pissarro did not decorate them with ornate patterns or designs, preferring full compositional narratives. It is, however,

The Turkey Girl, 1885. Fan painted in gouache.

not certain whether the fans produced by Degas and Pissarro were regarded as an extension of their paintings and drawings, or whether they did serve a utilitarian purpose.

These fresh involvements in Pissarro's life can be closely related to the stylistic difficulties that he was experiencing at the end of the 1870s. The technical experiments in printing enabled him to find a means of seeking clarity in complicated compositions. The printmaker concentrates very much on small areas, both on the intrinsic merits of the respective parts of the surface and on the way in which they relate to the whole design. Similarly, the curved shape of the fan forced the artist to concentrate on the relationship between foreground and background. The two corners had to be related to the central part of the fan so that the composition would be unified. Pissarro was also able to purify the surfaces of his densely worked canvases of the late 1870s by handling media that in themselves possessed different textural qualities. Pastel and gouache complemented one another in that the first was crumbly and the second smooth, whilst tempera partook of both qualities. Pissarro's sudden concentration on these media, no doubt encouraged by Degas, facilitated his handling of oil paint. Where *Côte des Bœufs* (1877) and the related landscapes of those years are almost embossed with paint, their surfaces corrugated with ribbed panels, the paintings of the early 1880s are executed in smaller, more even strokes directed in precisely defined directions. Interestingly, later in the 1880s during his Neo-Impressionist phase, Pissarro again sought an antidote to the discipline of his current style, this time finding relief in watercolour. Recourse to technical experimentation, therefore, assisted him during the critical years of 1879–1882. By modifying his style, he was able to achieve the clarity on the surface of the canvas that he felt he had gradually lost during the second half of the 1870s.

The first half of the 1880s was also a period when, as regards subject matter, Pissarro widened his terms of reference. His interest in Rouen epitomizes this broadening of interest, incorporating both topography and caricature. His fascination for the city of Rouen was kindled by a protracted visit made in 1883, which led to long and productive painting campaigns there in 1896 and 1898. There are countless references to Rouen in Pissarro's letters of these years, which, together with references in Julie Manet's diary, provide a vivid account of his activities in the city. In October 1896 he wrote to his eldest son, "It is as beautiful as Venice... it has extraordinary character and is really beautiful." This is the key to the significance of Rouen in Pissarro's art. In both Venice and Rouen there was a similar contrast between past and present, symbolized by the historic architecture and a modern working port. There was a similar magic in the effects derived from the aesthetic relationship between buildings and water—in Rouen the Seine, in Venice the lagoon and canals. Above all, both Rouen and Venice had well established topographical traditions that could be readily exploited. In short, for Pissarro Rouen was a much larger version of Pontoise, but, more importantly, it was a place he could exploit more readily.

The topographical tradition of Rouen falls into two broad categories. The first may be termed the antiquarian, enshrined in Baron Taylor's monumental *Voyages pittoresques et romantiques dans l'ancienne France* (1820-1878), which had three volumes devoted to Normandy. It is, of course, with the *Voyages pittoresques* that the much respected Richard Bonington was associated, executing lithographs of the rue du Gros-Horloge in Rouen and of the large church of Saint-Gervais-et-Saint-Protais in Gisors. Pissarro, too, responded to the "*motifs pittoresques*" that he found in Rouen and Gisors and gave expression to them almost solely in the traditional form of prints. Pissarro notes in his letters the changes in the rue du Gros-Horloge since the publication of Bonington's print and later in February 1896, when contemplating making a lithograph of the rue Saint-Romain in Rouen, he expresses his desire in a letter to make "some sketches of old streets which are being destroyed." Such an attitude, as well as his admiration for

Richard Parkes Bonington (1802-1828).
Rue du Gros-Horloge, Rouen. Lithograph from Baron Taylor,
Voyages pittoresques et romantiques dans l'ancienne France.

the famous late Gothic wooden sculptures that adorned the exteriors of the houses, place Pissarro firmly within the antiquarian fold.

The second category of the topographical tradition of Rouen is more pictorial. It is enshrined in the engravings after the watercolours of J.M.W. Turner, published in his *Annual Tour – The Seine* (1834), which dominate the guide book literature for the rest of the nineteenth century. The tourist was encouraged to

J.M.W. Turner (1775-1851).
View of Rouen. Engraving from Annual Tour – The Seine, *1834.*

view the city of Rouen from two spectacular vantage points. The first lay to the north-east of the city from Bonsecours on Mont Sainte-Catherine, of which J.S. Cotman, J.M.W. Turner, Corot and Théodore Rousseau, among many others, had made records, while Pissarro limited himself to a single deftly executed drawing. The second view lay on the other side of the city to the north-west seen from the village of Canteleu. Pissarro visited Canteleu in October 1883 in the presence of Monet and Durand-Ruel. "We beheld the most wonderful landscape a painter could hope to see. The view of Rouen in the distance with the Seine spread out as calm as glass, sunny slopes, splendid foregrounds, was magical." Although his stated intention was to record this view, Pissarro did not actually do so and we cannot, therefore, compare his result with those by J.M.W. Turner, Paul Huet, Corot, or Monet. It might be thought that Pissarro's comparative reluctance to paint or draw these traditional views of Rouen divorces him from that particular tradition, whereas, in fact, he seems, perhaps unconsciously, to have allied himself to a later development of it.

The character of the Seine had changed enormously with the development of modern modes of travel, such as trains and steamers, which had a particular significance for Impressionist painters. The railway from Paris to Le Havre took 4-5 hours by a fast train; the steamer took 9-10 hours from Le Havre to Rouen and then a further 13 hours to Paris. The steamer only operated between April and November, while the trains offered a far more varied service. These new forms of transport are absorbed into the topographical and guide book literature, as can be seen in the vignette illustrations to Jules Janin's *La Normandie* (1844), two of which make interesting comparisons with works by Monet and Pissarro. The comparison between the vignette of the quayside at Rouen with Pissarro's etchings of the Cours Boieldieu suggests that as an artist it was the genre-like aspects of the city that absorbed him rather than the general views. This conclusion is also valid for the prints of the streets and port of Rouen, and it enabled Pissarro to combine topography with caricature, this last being an integral part of his art. Yet, the character of Rouen had changed profoundly. The

The Quayside at Rouen, 1883.

semi-rural flavour of the Cours-la-Reine, or the charms of the Ile Lacroix had been almost totally overwhelmed by industrialization. The map published in Baedeker's *Guide* of 1899 shows very clearly the changing character of the city. The concentration of medieval streets, churches, buildings, and markets lies around the cathedral on the north side of the Seine. Because of this particular focus, the *boulevards* circle the outside of the city culminating in the Cours Boieldieu, which was the most fashionable street in the city. The *quais* formed the main artery of Rouen and witnessed its transformation into a deep-water inland port with easy access to Paris, which, during the 1890s, handled as many as 5,000

Cours Boieldieu, Rouen, 1884. Etching.

ships per annum. It is the industrial appearance of Rouen in contrast with its medieval heritage that came increasingly to exercise Pissarro. The bridges (Pont Corneille and Pont Boieldieu), the industrial quarter of Saint-Sever to the south, the factories and warehouses on the islands of Lacroix and Brouilly, are all frequently depicted in Pissarro's paintings of the 1890s, as opposed to the west façade of the cathedral, which was executed, amongst others, by J.S. Cotman, J.M.W. Turner, Léon Lhermitte and, definitively, by Monet. At first, in 1883, Pissarro approached the theme of industrialized Rouen with due caution, deciding possibly that his detailed style of painting was not the right one for the type of picture he wanted to paint. For this he had to wait until the 1890s and some of these paintings will be discussed in the final chapter. Pissarro, therefore, fed on the images that he recorded in 1883 and continued to make prints of the old and the modern Rouen for the rest of the decade.

The Sorting of Cabbages, 1883-1895.

The caricatural element in Pissarro's art is perhaps more apparent in his depiction of the local markets held at Pontoise and Gisors. The first market scenes date from 1881 and were subsequently executed more often in gouache, tempera and pastel, as opposed to oil. Numerous drawings testify to his close observation of these important social scenes and Pissarro seems particularly to have enjoyed observing the intermingling of different social classes. "Don't strive for skilful line, strive for simplicity, for the essential lines which give the physiognomy. Rather incline towards caricature than towards prettiness," was how he advised Lucien Pissarro to draw the human figure in a letter of July 1883. In his market scenes Pissarro displays a host of different types recording them first in his sketchbooks before incorporating them into more finished works. These last are a development of those market scenes dating from the birth of genre painting in the Netherlands and Italy at the beginning of the seventeenth century. Pissarro, however, concentrates very much on the social implications of a market and on the transactions made between people. He does not seize the opportunity to execute a series of still lifes and even in *The Pork Butcher* it is not the meat that he draws attention to, so much as the position of the figures within the framework of the stalls and their relationship one to another. In Pissarro's œuvre the market scenes form a small, though coherent, group of images, like the bathers of the 1890s. It is the socio-economic aspects that seem initially to have attracted him to the subject, but, ultimately, the market became an elaborate exercise in the treatment of the human figure.

These various strands in Pissarro's activity during the early part of the 1880s may, at first, appear to be rather disparate, but, in fact, they form the basis of those most important paintings undertaken between 1880-1885. These paintings are of great consequence for those artists of the younger generation who oscillated towards Pissarro during the 1880s, especially Gauguin and Van Gogh. The paintings differ vastly from those of the 1870s in their treatment of the human figure. Before, the figures form only a single unit in the composition. The artist records their activities, but relates them directly to the surroundings. During the 1880s,

Poultry Market at Pontoise, 1882.

Vegetable Market, Pontoise, 1891. Etching.

The Pork Butcher, 1883.

Young Woman Washing Dishes, 1882.

Peasant Woman with Hand on Hip, c. 1881.

however, Pissarro places far less emphasis on the background and far more on the figure itself. The setting becomes little more than a backdrop against which the figures are offset. This meant that there was far less concentration on spatial recession and depth, since the figures were placed prominently in the foreground and often seen from oblique angles. There is less reliance on outline, each form being treated identically with small even brushstrokes, so that there is no real differentiation between various parts of the surface of the canvas. Pissarro's new found technical sophistication allowed him to camouflage the figures amidst their surroundings without, however, in any way sacrificing the sense of form, or the solidity of the human frame. This readiness to depict the human figure was becoming apparent towards the end of the 1870s in such paintings as *Woman cleaning a Saucepan*, but the boldness with which the figures now fill the composition and are placed in the immediate foreground, often cut off at the edge, perhaps belies outside influences, such as the spatial ambiguity of Degas, the increasing importance of photography, or even of Japanese prints, which also interested Pissarro at this time and increasingly so during the 1890s. The drawings made by Pissarro at the beginning of the 1880s confirm all of these tendencies.

Kitagawa Utamaro (1753-1806). The Courtesan Kisegawa of the Teahouse Matsuba-ya, from the series A Competition of Five Lovely Women.

Young Peasant Woman taking her Coffee, 1881.

Peasant Women Resting, 1881.

Study for The Harvest. *Black chalk and watercolour.*

Compositional study for The Harvest. *Brush drawing in grey wash.*

Study of Two Female Harvesters, 1882. Black chalk.

Landscape drawings are often reduced to formulae, whilst there is a proliferation of powerful figure studies made from life and from posed models. In these studies Pissarro explores a variety of postures and activities. The rhythmical outlines, frequently redrawn, evince his obvious pleasure in the rounded forms of the human figure.

The climax of this particular phase in Pissarro's art is marked by the seventh Impressionist exhibition (1882) at which he exhibited over thirty pictures, most of them incorporating his new treatment of the human figure. In fact, these pictures are somewhat surprising for an artist who is so often regarded as a landscape painter. In this respect, Pissarro moved closer to Degas and Renoir—the supreme figure painters of the Impressionist group. The preparatory methods used for the tempera of *The Harvest* (1882), which was also included in the seventh Impressionist exhibition, accords well with Degas' oft quoted statement that there was nothing spontaneous about his art. *The Harvest* shows a large field near Pontoise. The long horizon is relieved by the slight rise at the left where a few houses are situated. The horizon is placed high up in the picture space, so that most of the surface is devoted to the expanse of field. There is a zig-zag progression within the composition along the horizon leading to the cart, the stooping figures in the middle distance, and the female harvester in the lower left corner, who walks towards and almost past the viewer out of the picture. Pissarro prepared this tempera in a number of drawings beginning with a general view of the field and numerous independent studies of harvesters at work. The actual formulation of the composition was established most probably in the studio, where individual poses are also refined before appearing in the final painting. The gradual accumulation of visual data relating to a single theme and the elaborate refinement of poses matches Degas' own working methods and intense application in the preparation of a composition.

Pissarro's figures also have a certain psychological introspection that can be found in the subject matter treated by Degas. In contrast with the 1870s, the figures in Pissarro's paintings of the early 1880s are immobile, or, alternatively, pursue gentle tasks. They sit, lie, or

The Harvest, 1882. Tempera.

loll on the ground, chatting, resting or reflecting. It is as though, having decided to enlarge the figure within the composition, Pissarro wants to focus attention on the inner state of mind, as opposed to the outward activity. Compositionally, however, these paintings owe a great deal to Renoir, whose mastery of the human figure first dates from the late 1860s but re-emerged during the early 1880s. Pissarro's regard for Renoir's painting is often discounted, owing to their political differences, but there are undeniable connections between some of Renoir's paintings of the 1870s and Pissarro's figure paintings of 1879-1882. The placement of the figure in the front of the picture, the angle at which it is viewed, the disruption of traditional spatial unity, and, above all, the effect of dappled light spread over figure and background alike, or the light-filled atmosphere, reveal a kinship with Renoir's *The Swing* and *Le Moulin de la Galette* (1876) or *Woman's Torso in Sunlight* (1875-1876).

It is characteristic of Pissarro that even in his most radical phase his work can be closely related to tradition. *Portrait of a Young Woman wearing a Hat* (1881) possesses a purity of form that evokes comparison with the Italian Renaissance. The demure pose of the girl with her hands clasped in her lap suggests a Raphaelesque madonna, whereas the conical shape of the hat recalls Piero della Francesca. There is no documentary evidence to suggest that Pissarro had these two particular artists in mind and he might just as easily have learnt similar lessons from examining paintings by Corot and Ingres, but there is, none the less, an awareness of tradition. There is also an intimation of the future in that the purity of form anticipates the figures of Seurat and the simplicity of the pose might have inspired Van Gogh in the last year of his life at Auvers-sur-Oise, while the rounded form anticipates aspects of Matisse's portraiture. A similar historical dimension may be observed at work in a painting like *The Little Country Maid* (1882) which, by virtue of its subject, prompts comparison with Dutch seventeenth-century interiors. On the other hand, the delicate interplay between the vertical lines of the doorway and walls, the horizontal lines of the top of the panelling and picture frames, and the round edge of the table promote a feeling of spatial disequilibrium. Where the seventeenth-century artist

Raphael (1483-1520).
La Belle Jardinière, c. 1507.

Vincent Van Gogh (1853-1890). Peasant Woman
seated against a Background of Wheat, 1890.

Henri Matisse (1869-1954).
Girl in White, 1919.

Young Peasant Woman wearing a Hat, 1881.

February, Sunrise, Bazincourt, 1893.

Eragny-sur-Epte, a small village near Gisors, off the Paris-Dieppe road, where Pissarro had rented a large house with grounds in 1884. With some financial help from Monet, Pissarro was able to buy the house in 1892 and to convert a substantial barn in the garden into his studio. The studio overlooked an orchard and beyond that the meadows leading to the neighbouring village of Bazincourt. Pissarro, now aged and suffering almost constantly from an eye complaint known as dacryocystitis, became more sedentary and frequently had to observe motifs from behind protected positions. Yet, like Monet at Giverny, Pissarro's examination of the rural spectacles that surrounded him was intense. He luxuriated in the changing temporal conditions and found the fogs, frosts and snow of winter or the vibrant warmth and lush verdure of summer equally rewarding. Pissarro also began to paint in series, restlessly altering his position or line of vision, but relying basically for his visual variety on the changing seasons or the divisions of the day. It is interesting that Pissarro's terms of reference for painting in series were therefore somewhat wider than those chosen by Monet, implying that his search for totality was of a different order.

The late rural paintings of Pissarro were particularly admired by Georges Lecomte who, on several occasions, wrote eulogistically about them. "If the painter powerfully elucidates the fecundity of the soil, the germinations, the luxuriant growths, and the noble breadth of the earth's modulations, he always populates his fertile fields and his meadows with active peasants and living animals. Creatures and objects emerge with a shining clarity: the air circulates around them; dazzling vapours of gold cast haloes around them. It is the glorious rapture of nature dressed overall. If it is either the rust-coloured frisson of autumn, or the harsh breeze that cracks the deep layers of snow, there is always the calming sense of space, so silent, and without any disturbance other than that, so appropriately harmonizing, of the star throwing out its light. It is the essence of the countryside, the spirit of the fields that these melodious symphonies reveal."

View of Eragny-sur-Epte, 1885.

Plum Trees in Flower at Eragny-sur-Epte, 1894.

Two Young Peasant Women in Conversation, 1892.

The compositions of these rural paintings mark a resolution of that constant dialogue in Pissarro's work between the figure and the setting. While *Two Young Peasant Women* (1892) returns to the devices of the early 1880s with the half-length figures placed prominently against the picture plane, it also shows the degree of confidence with which Pissarro could now handle the human figure. He was, however, not to explore this type of composition further, preferring instead to insert the figure into a specific setting, as opposed to allowing it to dominate. This, in turn, meant a return to a more

Old Ramparts (The Path), 1889.

The Gardener, Afternoon Sun, Eragny-sur-Epte, 1899.

Haymakers, Eragny-sur-Epte, Evening, 1893.

The same devices can be detected at work in *The Haymaking, Eragny-sur-Epte* (1901), where the foreground is marked by the figure leaning against the tree on the right and the middle distance by the foliage on the left, before the eye escapes towards the rest of the field in the background. The figures in both these paintings are not always realized with the greatest success. Some of the gestures appear wooden, but it has to be remembered that Pissarro was composing these canvases in an additive way, assembling the figures one by one, sometimes taking them from different contexts. What is important, however, is that the scale of the figures is gauged to the setting. There is no tension between the background and the foreground. One is not sacrificed to the other, and Pissarro achieves several compositions at this late stage of his life where the figures assume equal importance with the elements of the landscape. Yet, it will be observed that the figures are nearly always placed in the foreground or the middle distance. Furthermore, they frequently work or rest within enclosed areas—meadows, orchards, fields, shady bowers, walled gardens. Pissarro cloisters his figures within a bounded demesne, almost a Garden of Eden. Why he does this will be discussed later in this chapter.

traditional system of perspective, even though a sense of distance is achieved not by a single vanishing point, but by horizontal strips in front of which the figures work, relax or bathe. Distance is established by *repoussoir* motifs extending inwards from the edges of the composition like stage flats. In *Haymakers, Evening, Eragny-sur-Epte* (1893), first the haystack on the left and then the tree on the right mark the distances back into the painting behind which the background can be seen.

The Artist's Garden at Eragny-sur-Epte, 1898.

Haymaking, Eragny-sur-Epte, 1901.

Washerwomen, Eragny, 1895.

Peasant Girl bathing her Legs, 1895.

Female Bathers Wrestling. Lithograph.

Francesco Albani (1578-1660). Diana and Actaeon.

Perhaps the most surprising demonstration of this private world is Pissarro's sudden preoccupation with the female nude. Although there are some isolated drawings dating from the early 1880s of female bathers, they are very much in the manner of Cézanne and it is known that Pissarro owned one of Cézanne's paintings of this subject. Pissarro himself only attempted the theme in the 1890s when Cézanne's work was beginning to be shown in Paris, and, in fact, produced many more prints, mainly lithographs, of bathers than paintings. His attitude was equivocal. In July 1893 he wrote to Lucien, "I have also prepared several compositions of Peasant Girls Bathing in a clear stream under a shade of willows; this tropical heat suggests motifs of shaded spots on river banks. It seems to me that I have the best sense of the great poetry in this. What hampers me is the impossibility of getting a model, otherwise I could do things which would be new and rare." The lithographs Pissarro referred to in April 1894 as "in romantic styles which seemed to me to have a rather amusing side: *Baigneuses*, plenty of them, in all sorts of poses, in all sorts of paradises. Interiors, too, Peasant Women at their Toilette etc. Such are the motifs I work on when I can't go outdoors." On the other hand, Pissarro was afraid of causing offence, describing two of his etchings of nude female bathers as "perhaps too naturalistic,

Two Female Bathers, 1894. Etching.

Female Bather, 1895.

these are peasant women—in hearty nakedness! I am afraid it will offend the delicate" (January 1894).

When examined, Pissarro's *Bathers* are difficult to analyse and it is with art-historical tradition rather than Cézanne or Degas that the chief comparisons are to be found. Marcantonio Raimondi, Italian baroque painting, Rembrandt and Boucher are artists to whose works Pissarro may have referred in the context of this particular theme. Of these, the reference to Rembrandt is documented, while knowledge of Boucher may originally have come through Cézanne, who possessed a photograph of Boucher's *Diana at the Bath*, a painting in the Musée du Louvre at that time. There are also

hints in the triad of figures found in some of the *Bathers* that Pissarro was painting a modern variant of the *Three Graces*. It is perfectly possible that he had a classical source in mind during this period, because he was preparing illustrations for *Daphnis and Chloë* with Lucien and the question of how to treat the nude for this famous pastoral romance frequently arose in correspondence. With this in mind, it is possible to regard Pissarro's *Bathers* as marking a half-way stage between those mythological themes painted by artists of earlier centuries and the earthly paradise depicted by the Fauves. Pissarro therefore, in the treatment of this subject, stands, like Hercules, at the crossroads.

The second group of paintings that dominates Pissarro's late works is the cityscapes or urban scenes. These were by no means limited to Paris, but included numerous paintings of Rouen, Dieppe and Le Havre. Strictly speaking, these last cannot be called cityscapes, for they concentrate, for the most part, on the port of Rouen and the harbours of Dieppe and Le Havre. As such, they are basically marine industrial scenes. Certainly no other Impressionist painter dedicated himself so earnestly to the task of depicting industrial views, just as no other Impressionist painter made such an intense study of Paris. These aspects of Pissarro's late work are rarely given the emphasis they deserve and yet they counteract the simplified designation of the artist working solely as a landscape painter. Pissarro began his views of Paris in 1893 when he painted the Place du Havre from the Hôtel Garnier opposite the Gare Saint-Lazare. It was not until 1897 that he concentrated upon the boulevards, selecting the Boulevard Montmartre, as seen from the Grand Hôtel de Russie (1, rue Drouot), as the main motif. A year later he established himself in the Hôtel du Louvre, situated on the Place du Palais-Royal, from where he observed the rue Saint-Honoré, the Avenue de l'Opéra and the Place du Théâtre-Français. Three other locations in Paris also served as bases for painting campaigns during the artist's final years: apartments on the rue de Rivoli (No. 204) overlooking the Jardin des Tuileries and at 28, Place Dauphine on the Ile de la Cité overlooking the Seine with the Pont Neuf in the immediate foreground, and, finally, a room in the Hôtel du Quai Voltaire on the left bank of the Seine. In each of these locations Pissarro remained above street level, partly for medical reasons owing to his eye infection, but, none the less, to great compositional advantage. It is significant that he painted his views of Paris in series, subjecting the boulevards and avenues to the same careful scrutiny as the orchard and meadow at Eragny-sur-Epte. In short, Pissarro brought a similar degree of concentration to both rural and urban subjects.

Perhaps the most important aspect of Pissarro's urban paintings is their composition. The viewer is forced to "read" the picture from the lower edge upwards. The eye is drawn up the boulevard or avenue,

Place du Havre, Paris, 1893.

Boulevard Montmartre, Winter Morning, 1897.
La Place du Théâtre-Français, Rain, 1898.

La Place du Carrousel, Afternoon Sun, 1899.

placed either on a diagonal or at right angles to the picture plane. Pissarro has increased this effect of telescoping by splaying out the buildings on either side and by exaggerating slightly the size of the Opéra at the end of the Avenue de l'Opéra, or of the lamppost and trees in the middle of the Boulevard Montmartre. Even the horizontal accents derived mainly from architectural elements are used to assist the eye in its plunge further into the city. Yet, the feeling of recession is not the same as that employed for the Route de Versailles during the early 1870s where Pissarro has adopted a system of one point perspective. Here recession is flattened out on the canvas to create a patterned fabric of movement within a closely defined space. The eye becomes absorbed by the flow of traffic and by the progress of the pedestrians crossing the street or walking on the pavements. Furthermore, the focus of each of the paintings of the Avenue de l'Opéra changes slightly with the repositioning of the roundabout in the Place du Théâtre-Français. Pissarro's radical redeployment of perspective in the boulevards and avenues paintings, perhaps

Tuileries Gardens, 1900.
Pont-Neuf, 1901.

The Pont-Royal and the Pavillon de Flore, 1903.

Avenue de l'Opéra, Sun on a Winter Morning, 1898.

Place du Théâtre-Français, Sun, 1898.

Boulevard Montmartre, Mardi Gras, 1897.

St. John's Bay®

MEN'S ST. JOHN'S BAY® POLOS
Orig. 26.00.

derived from Japanese prints, results in a feeling of disjunction or dislocation, which, in turn, promotes a sense of movement or internal rhythm within each canvas. The spectator searching out details on the surface of these paintings becomes disorientated, as could so easily happen on the street itself. If single figures are examined, whether they walk up the Avenue de l'Opéra, in the Jardin des Tuileries, or across the Pont Neuf, it will be seen that their forms merge with the background, occasionally becoming mere ciphers represented only by a blurred anonymity. Of the motif of the Avenue de l'Opéra Pissarro wrote to Lucien in December 1897, "I forgot to mention that I found a room in the Grand Hôtel du Louvre with a superb view of the Avenue de l'Opéra and the corner of the Place du Palais-Royal. It is very beautiful to paint. Perhaps it is not aesthetic, but I am delighted to be able to paint these Paris streets that people have come to call ugly, but which are so silvery, so luminous and vital. They are so different from the *boulevards*. This is completely modern!"

The Place du Théâtre-Français, 1898.

Ando Hiroshige (1797-1858).
Otsu, No. 54, Village Street in Early Spring,
with Printseller's Shop.

-1944).

Pierre Bonnard (1867-1947).
Narrow Street in Paris or Rue Tholozé.

Pissarro painted and exhibited his views of Paris in series, examining each one from his vantage point at different times of day under different weather conditions over relatively short periods. There is a remarkable vigour in these paintings. The choice of subject was audacious, the compositional difficulties formidable and the relevant technical skills considerable. Yet, Pissarro succeeded in this difficult task and in doing so prompts comparisons with the work of a host of different artists. The vantage point above street level and the redeployment of perspective, for instance, recur in the work of Bonnard and Vuillard. It has also been claimed that the "accidental strewing of figures and vehicles" is "analogous to the multitude of single and clustered bars in Mondrian's abstractions," while, spiritually, there is perhaps a kinship with Edvard Munch's attitude to urban spaces. Another surprising element in Pissarro's urban views is the application of colour. The three paintings of the Boulevard Montmartre at Mardi-Gras, dating from 1897, are loosely executed, but the most highly finished has a density of fresh, high-keyed colour in the centre of the composition that might almost have been squeezed straight from the tube onto the canvas.

Sunset, the Port of Rouen (Smoke), 1898.

J.M.W. Turner (1775-1851). Dido Building Carthage, 1815.

A similar vitality characterizes the pictures of Rouen, Dieppe and Le Havre. These were painted intermittently with the Paris views. Again Pissarro used hotels, or rooms overlooking the bustling scenes of port or harbour. He then proceeded to dissect the scene presented by his vantage points, altering his line of vision slightly within any one given direction. In Rouen he began work in 1896 in the Hôtel de Paris (51, quai de Paris) before moving to the Hôtel d'Angleterre in the Cours Boieldieu. From these hotels he could examine the loading and unloading of ships, the traffic moving across the bridges and the activity on the quayside. Before him lay the waters of the Seine punctuated by ships, as well as extensive views of bridges, warehouses, factories and the Gare d'Orléans—all of which symbolized the industrial expansion of the city. Even when faced with modernity, however, Pissarro had recourse to tradition. *Sunset, the Port of Rouen (Smoke)*, of 1898, for instance, is a subject that evokes comparison with Claude and Turner. Indeed, Pissarro refers to the juxtaposition of two appropriate paintings by these artists in the National Gallery, London (*The Embarkation of the Queen of Sheba* by Claude and *Dido building Carthage* by Turner), which he must have known, since in May 1902 he advises Lucien to go and look at them. By contrast, when Pissarro turned away from the river towards the old part of Rouen nestling around the cathedral, he again chose an unusual viewpoint from the Hôtel de Paris looking over the rooftops towards the south side of the cathedral. Only one view in Rouen painted by Pissarro during the 1890s can be regarded as an updating of the established topographical tradition. This is of the Rue de l'Epicerie from the Place de la Haute-Vieille-Tour looking towards the south portal of the cathedral known as the Portail de la Calende. Like Monet in 1892, Pissarro positions himself by the Place de la Fierté from where Samuel Prout had also depicted the scene at the beginning of the nineteenth century. Where, however, Prout has stressed the medieval aspects of the composition, Pissarro's paintings of the Rue de l'Epicerie have an inner strength derived from the interlocking of architectural motifs and the strong verticals of the cathedral seen in the background. He thus evokes contemporary life in the city, as opposed to

Rue de l'Epicerie, Rouen, 1898.

The Fair at Dieppe, Sunshine, Afternoon, 1901.

*Photograph of
Camille Pissarro
about 1895.*

144

List of Illustrations

The following catalogue references are used for individual works listed below: PV (Ludovic Rodo Pissarro and Lionello Venturi, *Camille Pissarro, son art, son œuvre*, a catalogue raisonné in two volumes, Paul Rosenberg, Paris, 1939); BL (Richard Brettell and Christopher Lloyd, *Catalogue of the Drawings by Camille Pissarro in the Ashmolean Museum*, Oxford, 1980); D (Loys Delteil, *Le Peintre Graveur illustré*, Vol. XVII, Paris, chez l'auteur, 1923; reprinted, New York, Collectors Edition, 1970); W (Georges Wildenstein, *Gauguin*, Paris, 1964); V (Lionello Venturi, *Cézanne, son art, son œuvre*, a catalogue raisonné in two volumes, Paul Rosenberg, Paris, 1936).

PISSARRO: TEMPERA AND GOUACHE

PISSARRO: DRAWINGS AND PRINTS

PHOTOGRAPHS

Index of Names and Places

HINSDALE PUBLIC LIBRARY
HINSDALE, IL 60521

PUBLISHED SEPTEMBER 1981
PICTURE EDITOR LAURO VENTURI
ILLUSTRATIONS BY LITH-ART, BERN
PRINTED BY IMPRIMERIES RÉUNIES, LAUSANNE
BINDING BY MAYER & SOUTTER, RENENS/LAUSANNE

PRINTED IN SWITZERLAND